DRACULA

DRACULA

by Bram Stoker

adapted for the stage by

Jane Thornton and John Godber

WARNER/CHAPPELL PLAYS

LONDON

A Warner Music Group Company

Jane Thornton was runner-up in the Sunday Times Playwriting Competition with her play *Simple Game* in 1984. She has since written *Amidst the Standing Corn* for Joint Stock Theatre Company, and her other plays include *Back to the Walls, Cut and Dried* and *Catwalk*. Together with John Godber Jane has co-written *Everyday Heroes* and *Shakers*, which has been produced worldwide. She has also written the musical and television versions of *Shakers*, and co-written the BBC series *Bloomin' Marvellous* with John Godber. She has written the film *It's Happy Hour Again* for Channel 4 television and plays for BBC radio including *It's A Lovely Day Tomorrow* and *Bully*. Jane is also a director and as an actor has appeared in numerous roles on stage and television.

John Godber was born in Yorkshire in 1956. A trained teacher with an MA in drama, it was whilst teaching from 1981-83 that he gained national recognition winning major awards at the National Student Drama Festival and at the Edinburgh Festival. His stage plays include *Bouncers, The Office Party, On the Piste, Up 'N' Under, Cramp, Blood, Sweat and Tears, September in the Rain, Happy Jack, Teechers, Salt of the Earth, Happy Families, April in Paris, Passion Killers, Lucky Sods, Gym and Tonic* and *Weekend Breaks*. With Jane Thornton he has co-written the play *Shakers*. He has also written extensively for television including numerous episodes of *Crown Court, Grange Hill* and *Brookside*, the six part BBC series *The Ritz* and it's sequel *The Continental* and the screenplay *My Kingdom For A Horse*. John has also devised and written two series for BBC television, *Chalkface* and *Bloomin' Marvellous*, and has written and directed the feature film version of *Up 'N' Under*.

DRACULA
First published in 1998
by Warner/Chappell Plays Ltd
Griffin House, 161 Hammersmith Road, London W6 8BS

ISBN 0 85676 216 4

Printed by Commercial Colour Press, London E7

DRACULA was first presented by Hull Truck Theatre Company on 25th October, 1995 at the Hull Truck Theatre, Hull, with the following cast:

COUNT DRACULA/ RENFIELD	Robert Angell
PROFESSOR VAN HELSING	Peter Cleall
LUCY WESTENRA	Melissa Collier
JONATHAN HARKER/ ARTHUR HOLMWOOD	Dominic Curtis
DR JOHN SEWARD	Paul Gilmore
MINA HARKER	Zoe Lucker

All other parts played by the ensemble.

Directed by Graham Watts
Designed by Alison Taylor
Lighting design by George Morris
Original Music by Carl Hogarth

ACT ONE

*The action takes place on what is essentially an empty stage.
A few old chairs, upstage a raised area connected by ramps.
Candles, cobwebs, a plethora of coffins. There are also areas
for the actors to sit behind and conceal themselves. The
actors come on stage and take up their positions,* JONATHAN
HARKER *standing centre stage. He has a suitcase with him.*

Silence.

HARKER	I left Munich at 8.35PM, May 1st.
VOICE 1	Arrived Vienna early next morning.
VOICE 4	Budapest is wonderful.
VOICE 2	Transylvania and Moldavia . . .
VOICE 3	. . . are in the midst of the Carpathians.
HARKER	One of the wildest and least known places in Europe.

> (*Music. Mist. We get the impression that*
> HARKER *is in a coach heading for Castle
> Dracula. The other actors also move and
> chastise their imaginary horses.*)

VOICE 1	Garrrrgghh . . . (*Charging his horses.*)
VOICE 2	Velcome to the Carpathians . . . (*Laughter.*)
VOICE 3	Must you go, young Herr, must you go . . . ?
VOICE 4	Do you know what day it is . . . ?
HARKER	It is the eve of St George's day!
VOICE 1	For your mother's sake don't go!
VOICE 2	Velcome to the Borgo Pass.

VOICE 3   Take a crucifix.

VOICE 4   Don't go . . . for God's sake come back . . .

VOICE 1   Velcome to Bukovina.

VOICE 2   Do you know what day it is . . . ?

VOICE 3   For your mother's sake . . .

VOICE 4   Velcome to Transylvania.

VOICE 1   Denn die todten reiten schnell . . .

VOICE 2   Denn die todten reiten schnell . . .

VOICE 3   Den die todten reiten schnell . . .

VOICE 4   The dead travel fast.

               (*The four actors fade and disappear into the
               hidden area of the set, upstage; all props and
               costumes are either hung or secreted about
               the setting.*)

HARKER   What sort of place had I come to? And among
               what kind of people? What sort of grim
               adventure was it on which I had embarked?

VOICE 4   The dead travel fast.

HARKER   Whilst in London I had some time at my
               disposal and I made a search amongst the
               books in the British Museum regarding
               Transylvania.

               (*Laughter.*)

               It struck me that some foreknowledge of that
               country might benefit me when dealing with a
               noble of that country. I was not able to find
               an exact location of the Castle Dracula, as
               there are no maps of this country as yet. And
               of bell or knocker there is equally no sign.

Was this a customary incident in the life of a solicitor's clerk? Solicitor's clerk! Mina wouldn't like that. Just before leaving London I recieved word that my examination was successful, and I am now a full-blown solicitor.

(*Laughter. From the darkness, a voice.*)

VOICE   (*off*) Mr Harker?

(*Slowly behind* HARKER, DRACULA *appears.*)

HARKER   Yes?

DRACULA   Welcome to my house. Enter freely of your own will! And please to leave something of the happiness you bring.

HARKER   Count Dracula?

DRACULA   I am Dracula. I bid you welcome Mr Harker. Come in. The night air is chill, and you must need to eat and rest. It is late and my people are not available. Allow me.

(DRACULA *takes* HARKER'S *cases off stage.*)

HARKER   I was led into a small occasional room lit by a single lamp, and without a window of any sort. Passing through this, he opened another door, and motioned me to enter. I rejoiced to see within a well-lit room a table which was spread for supper, and on whose mighty hearth a great fire of logs flamed and flared.

(DRACULA *enters.*)

DRACULA   You will find your supper prepared. I pray be seated. You will, I trust, excuse me that I don't join you. I have dined already.

(DRACULA *shows* HARKER *to his seat. His hand touches* HARKER, *who freezes for a moment —*

and then sits. Wolves howl in the distance.
HARKER *is startled.*)

HARKER   What the . . . ?

DRACULA   Listen to them — the children of the night.
                  What sweet music they make.

HARKER   Really?

DRACULA   Ah, you dwellers in the city cannot enter into
                  the feelings of the hunter.

HARKER   I think you may be right.

DRACULA   Eat.

HARKER   Yes. Are you sure you . . .

DRACULA   No, thank you. Your bedroom is ready, and
                  tomorrow you shall sleep as late as you will. I
                  unfortunately have to be away till the
                  afternoon; so sleep well.

HARKER   I will.

DRACULA   And dream well. Transylvania is a wonderful
                  place for dreams.

HARKER   Good night.

DRACULA   Good night.

                  (DRACULA *disappears upstage.* HARKER
                  addresses the audience.)

HARKER   I slept till late the next day, and woke of my
                  own accord. When I had finished breakfast I
                  looked for a bell so that I might let the
                  servants know I had finished — but I could
                  not find one. There are certainly odd
                  deficiencies in the house, considering the
                  extraordinary evidences of wealth which are
                  around me. There is not even a toilet glass on

my table, and I had to get the little shaving glass from my bag before I could shave. In fact there is absolutely nothing in the bedroom, no books, newspaper or even writing materials.

(*Laughter, off.*)

I made my way through the castle until I discovered . . .

(DRACULA *enters. We are now in the library.*)

DRACULA   I am glad you found your way in here.

HARKER   Books. Thousands of them. Books of the most varied kind — history, botany, geology, law — all relating to England and English life.

DRACULA   I am sure that there is much in the library to interest you.

HARKER   Yes, I was just . . .

DRACULA   Through these books I have come to know much about your great England; and to know her is to love her.

HARKER   Absolutely.

DRACULA   I long to go through the crowded streets of your mighty London, to be in the midst and the rush of humanity, to share it's life, it's change.

HARKER   Oh yes.

DRACULA   It's death.

HARKER   Oh.

DRACULA   And all that makes it what it is. But alas, as yet I only know your tongue through the books.

HARKER   But your English is wonderful.

DRACULA   You are too kind.

HARKER   Honestly.

DRACULA   I know that, did I move and speak in your London, none would know me. Here I am a noble. A boyar! The common people know me and I am a master. But a stranger in a strange land; he is no one. And to know not is to care not for.

HARKER   A stranger in a strange land.

DRACULA   You shall, I trust, rest here with me for a while, so that by our talking I may learn the English intonation; and I would that you tell me when I make an error, even the smallest, in my speaking.

HARKER   It doesn't seem fair.

DRACULA   Please, for me.

HARKER   I will of course, but . . .

DRACULA   I am sorry that I had to be away so long today; but you will, I know, forgive one who has so many important affairs in hand.

HARKER   Of course. I wonder if I may come into the library when I chose?

DRACULA   Yes certainly. You may go anywhere you wish in the castle, except where the doors are locked, where of course you will not wish to go. There is a reason that all things are as they are, and did you see with my eyes and know with my knowledge, you would perhaps better understand.

HARKER   Yes.

DRACULA   We are in Transylvania, and Transylvania is not England. (*Both men laugh*, HARKER *more nervously*.) Now you come to me not alone, but as agent of my friend Peter Hawkins of Exeter. So tell me of London and of the house you have procured for me.

HARKER   Ah yes . . . the estate is called Carfax.

DRACULA   Good.

HARKER   The house is very large and dates back to all periods. To medieval times even. One part of the stone is immensely thick, with only a few windows.

DRACULA   Very good.

HARKER   They are heavily barred with iron.

DRACULA   For safety?

HARKER   Absolutely.

DRACULA   And the location?

HARKER   There are only a few houses close at hand, one being a very large house only recently added to and formed into a private lunatic asylum. It is not however visible from the grounds. And nearby there is a church or chapel. I have taken a few Kodak views of it.

DRACULA   I am happy for this.

HARKER   It is a most exceptional property.

DRACULA   I am glad it is big and old. I am myself of an old family, and to live in a new house would kill me.

HARKER   The house is perfect.

DRACULA   I rejoice also that there is a chapel. We Transylvanian nobles love not to think that our bones may be amongst the common dead. The walls of my castle here are broken. The shadows are many, and the wind breathes cold. I love the shade and the shadows, and I care to be alone with my thoughts when I may.

HARKER   Yes yes, I understand.

DRACULA   And so I must go.

HARKER   Will we dine later?

DRACULA   (*sharply*) No. I am busy.

HARKER   Of course.

DRACULA   So many things to do, as I am sure you will understand.

HARKER   In preparation for your leaving?

DRACULA   Yes, yes of course. To my new home. So I go. Make yourself comfortable and we can talk again tomorrow. Goodbye. I look forward to talking further with you about my new country, England.

(DRACULA *exits*.)

HARKER   Somehow his words and his look did not seem to accord, or else it was that his cast of face made his smile look malignant and saturnine.

(*A beat*.)

I began to look at some of the books around me. One was an atlas which I found open, naturally, at England. Certain places were marked with rings around them. One was near London on the east side, certainly near where his new estate was, the other two were in

Exeter, and one was in Whitby on the
Yorkshire coast.

(*A beat.*)

VOICE 1   Velcome . . .

VOICE 2   To the Carpathians . . .

VOICE 3   Where the dead travel fast . . .

(*Music.* HARKER *takes out a bag, and begins to
shave. He holds up a mirror, so that he can
see himself. As he does this* DRACULA *enters.*
DRACULA *is not seen in the mirror. As* HARKER
turns and sees DRACULA, *he appears to cut
himself shaving.* DRACULA *makes a move
towards* HARKER. DRACULA *appears to be
salivating at the sight of the blood.*)

HARKER   Count Dracula . . .

DRACULA   Gut morning.

HARKER   Damn . . . cut my . . .

DRACULA   Yes.

HARKER   Damn . . .

DRACULA   Take care Mr Harker.

HARKER   I didn't see you come in. Sorry. I was
               thinking of dearest Mina . . .

DRACULA   Take care how you cut yourself. It is more
               dangerous than you think in this country.

               (DRACULA *picks up the shaving glass.*)

               And this is the wretched thing that has done
               the mischief?

HARKER   Yes, I couldn't find a mirror anywhere.

DRACULA   It's a foul bauble of man's vanity, is it not?
                 Away with it.

                 (DRACULA *takes the shaving mirror and
                 departs with a start upstage. He smashes the
                 mirror.*)

DRACULA   Smash, smash, smash into a thousand pieces.

                 (DRACULA *exits.*)

HARKER   The Count threw my shaving glass out of the
                 window where it fell and smashed into a
                 thousand pieces. What a quite extraordinary
                 fellow.

                 (*A beat.*)

                 Over breakfast I did a little exploring of the
                 castle. It is on the very edge of a terrible
                 precipice. A stone falling from the window
                 would fall a thousand feet without touching
                 anything! As far as the eye can see is a sea of
                 green tops, with occasionally a deep rift. Here
                 and there are silver threads where the rivers
                 wind in deep gorges through the forest. But I
                 am not in heart to describe such beauty, for
                 when I had seen the view I explored further:
                 doors, doors, doors everywhere, and all
                 locked and bolted.

VOICE 2   Velcome to Transylvania.

HARKER   In no place save from the windows in the
                 castle walls is there an available exit. The
                 castle is a veritable prison, and I a prisoner!

                 (HARKER *freezes where he is. Music. Blackout.
                 Two spotlights pick out* LUCY *and* MINA. *We
                 are in Whitby, Yorkshire. Each has a letter.
                 As they read they begin to acknowledge each
                 other.*)

LUCY	Dearest Lucy, forgive my long delay in writing. But I have simply been overwhelmed with work. The life of an assistant schoolmistress is sometimes trying.
MINA	My dearest Mina, you tax me very unfairly with being a bad correspondent. I wrote to you twice since we parted and your letter is only your second.
LUCY	I am longing to be with you, and by the sea.
MINA	We met, sometime ago, a man who would just do for you . . .
LUCY	I miss Jonathan greatly . . .
MINA	. . . if you were not already engaged to Jonathan.
LUCY	I hear rumours of a forthcoming marriage to a Mr Holmwood?
MINA	Rumours rumours, there are so many rumours. Arthur Holmwood is a charming lovely man, but only last week Mama and I met John Seward. He is a doctor, and very clever. He is only twenty nine and already has an immense lunatic asylum under his own care. He has the curious habit of looking one right in the eyes, as if he's trying to read your thoughts.
LUCY	I have just had a few hurried lines from Jonathan. Oh lucky Mina. You lucky girl. He is in Transylvania now and expects to return in a week.
MINA	Men are so noble. Mr Holmwood has approached me with an offer of marriage! Dr Seward, the lunatic man made a very cool approach to me last month, though I could see he was inwardly nervous.
LUCY	Johnathan is still away.

MINA   I don't know what to do.

LUCY   I miss him so. Yours, dearest Mina.

MINA   I love Arthur Holmwood, I love him. There.
                I've said it. We are to be married in the
                autumn.

LUCY   I wonder if he is thinking about me? Poor
                Mina.

MINA   I love him, I love him, I love him. Do you
                think that is silly of me? Forever, Lucy.

LUCY   You must come up to see me. This is such a
                lovely place. The little river, the Esk, runs
                through a deep valley. And right over the
                town is the ruin of the Abbey which was
                sacked by the Danes. There is a legend that a
                white lady is seen at one of the windows, and
                the graveyard there, is to my mind, the nicest
                spot. Please don't delay. Yours, darling Mina.
                Whitby, Yorkshire.

                (*Lights fade out on* LUCY *and* MINA. *Lights
                rise on* HARKER.)

HARKER   When I found I was a prisoner a sort of wild
                feeling came over me. I rushed up and down
                the stairs trying every door, and peering out
                of every window. But after a little time my
                helplessness overpowered all other things. I
                sat down and thought what had to be done.
                How was it that all the people in Bistritz had
                warned me of the count, how was it that the
                peasants at the coach inn had given me garlic,
                a crucifix and mountain ash. Bless that poor
                woman for whenever I touch it I glean some
                strength from its power.

VOICE 4   For your mother's sake don't go!

                (DRACULA *enters.*)

DRACULA   Have you written since your first letter to our
               friend Mr Peter Hawkins?

HARKER   No, not yet.

DRACULA   Or to any other?

HARKER   No, no.

DRACULA   Then write now, my young friend, write to
               our friend and to any other; and say, if it will
               please you, that you shall stay with me until a
               month from now.

HARKER   Do you wish me to stay so long?

DRACULA   I desire it much; nay, I take no refusal. When
               your master, employer, what you will,
               engaged that someone should come on his
               behalf, it was understood that my needs only
               were to be consulted. I have not stinted. Is it
               not so?

HARKER   Indeed not. But I thought I should go soon . . .

DRACULA   I pray you will not discourse of other things
               than your business in your letters. It will
               doubtless please your friends to know that you
               are well, and that you look forward to getting
               home to them. Is it not so?

HARKER   Count Dracula . . . ?

DRACULA   I trust you will forgive me, but I have much
               work to do in private. You will I hope find all
               things as you wish.

HARKER   I was wondering if I might . . .

DRACULA   Let me advise you my dear young friend —
               nay let me warn you with all seriousness, that
               should you leave these rooms you will not by
               any chance go to sleep in any other part of the

castle. It is old, and has many memories, and there are bad dreams for those who sleep unwisely.

(DRACULA *exits*.)

HARKER   When he left me I went to my room. After a while, not hearing any sound, I came out and went up the stone steps to where I could look out towards the south. As I leaned from the window my eye was caught by something moving a story below me.

(Music underscores the following.)

What I saw was the Count's head coming out of the window. I did not see the face, but I knew the man by the neck and the movement of his arms and back. I was at first interested. But my feelings changed to repulsion and terror when I saw the whole man slowly emerge from the window and crawl down the castle wall over that dreadful abyss, face down.

VOICE 3   (*whispers*) Oh my God!

HARKER   At first I could not believe my eyes. I thought it was some trick of the moon light, some weird effect of shadow but I kept looking and it could be no delusion. I saw the fingers and the toes grasp the corners of the stones, I saw him move, just like a lizard moves along a wall.

(Howls are heard, off.)

VOICE 1   (*whispers*) The dead travel fast.

HARKER   I feel the dread of this horrible place overpowering me; I am in fear, in awful fear — and there is no escape for me. I am trapped in terrors that I dare not even think of . . .

(*Music swells.* HARKER *moves upstage. He freezes, though we still see him in spotlight.* LUCY *enters, wearing only a translucent nightdress. She is clearly sleepwalking.* MINA, *also in her night shirt, is watching her.*)

MINA   Lucy . . . Lucy . . . Lucy . . . Lucy wake up . . . Lucy. Come back to bed dear. Lucy. Lucy, don't go near the windows Lucy, come back from the windows! Don't open the windows we are in for a storm tonight.

(LUCY *begins to laugh and sleepwalks her way across the stage and off.* MINA *follows her.* HARKER *comes back to life.*)

HARKER   Once more I have seen the Count go out in his lizard fashion. I knew he had left the castle now, and thought to use the opportunity to explore more than I had dared to as yet. At the top of a stairway, I found one door, though it seemed locked, give way a little under pressure. Here was an opportunity which I might not have again, and with many efforts I forced it back so I could enter. I slowly made my way down the narrow stairs . . .

(*A musical sting.*)

This was clearly a portion of the castle occupied in bygone days, the furniture had more of an air of comfort than I had seen. The windows were curtainless and the yellow moonlight, flooding in through the panes, enabled one to see even colours, whilst it softened the wealth of dust which lay over all and disguised in some measure the ravages of time.

(*A musical sting.*)

There was a dread of loneliness in the place which chilled my heart and made my nerves

tremble. Still it was better than living alone
in the rooms which I had come to hate from
the presence of the Count, and after trying to
school my nerves, I found a soft quietude
come over me. I felt sleepy. The Count's
warning came into mind, but I took a pleasure
in disobeying it. The sense of sleep was upon
me. I determined not to return tonight to the
gloomy haunted rooms, but to sleep here.

(*Music. As* HARKER *sleeps, a* VAMPIRE WOMAN
*enters. She is lustful and openly wanton. She
makes her way to* HARKER. *She begins to lick
his face. She arches like an animal. We see
the feline accent of her form. She licks his
neck and smacks her own lips. We notice that
she has large teeth. She arches back her neck
and makes a slow motion movement towards*
HARKER's *neck. She is just about to bite*
HARKER *when* DRACULA *appears.*)

DRACULA   How dare you — how dare you touch him
              when I have forbidden it! Back! This man
              belongs to me. He is mine. Beware how you
              meddle with him or you have to deal with me.

VAMPIRE   You? You have never loved anyone ever.

DRACULA   Yes I can, I too can love; you yourself can
              tell it from the past. Is it not so?

VAMPIRE   Who did you ever love?

DRACULA   I promise you that when I have finished with
              him you shall have him. Go go, go. There is
              much work to be done.

VAMPIRE   Am I to have nothing tonight?

DRACULA   Only this.

              (DRACULA *holds up a small black bag. The*
              VAMPIRE *looks in the bag.*)

VAMPIRE	A child?
	(*The* VAMPIRE *takes the bag and exits with a laugh.*)
DRACULA	Now go!!
HARKER	(*waking*) I was lost . . .
DRACULA	Yes, of course.
HARKER	The door opened and . . .
DRACULA	Tomorrow my friend we must part. You return to your beautiful England, I to some work which may have such an end we might never meet. I shall not be here but all shall be ready for your journey. In the morning come the Szgany, local gypsies who have labours of their own. When they have gone my carriage will come for you, and shall bear you to the Borgo Pass to meet the diligence from Bukovina to Bistritz. But I am in hopes that I shall see no more of you at Castle Dracula.
HARKER	May I not go tonight sir?
DRACULA	Not tonight.
HARKER	Why?
DRACULA	Because dear sir, my coachman is away on a mission.
HARKER	I would happily walk with pleasure.
DRACULA	No.
HARKER	I am in desperate need to get away at once.
DRACULA	And your baggage?
HARKER	I can send for it another time.

DRACULA   No.

HARKER   Please . . . please!

DRACULA   Come with me my dear young friend. Not an
               hour shall you wait in my house against your
               will, though sad I am at your going, and that
               you suddenly so desire it.

               (DRACULA *raises his hand. Wolves are heard.*)

HARKER   Wolves.

DRACULA   What sweet music they make.

HARKER   I er . . .

DRACULA   Goodbye.

HARKER   I think perhaps tonight is not the best time to
               depart. I should I think wait for your kind
               offer of a carriage.

DRACULA   Whatever you wish my young friend.

               (DRACULA *exits.*)

HARKER   No man knows till he has suffered from the
               night how sweet and how dear to his heart the
               morning can be. I must take some action now
               that the courage of the day is upon me. I have
               noted that it has always been at night time
               that I have been molested or threatened. I
               have not yet seen the Count in the daylight.
               Can it be that he sleeps while others wake? If
               I could only get into his room. But there is no
               way. No, there is a way. I will follow his
               lead. I will crawl from my window and enter
               through his. Goodbye Mina, if I fail. Goodbye
               all my faithful friends, goodbye all of you and
               last of all Mina.

MINA   Lucy! Lucy!

(Music. Upstage, a number of the coffins are brought into view. Though we cannot see into the coffins, DRACULA *is in one of them.* HARKER *makes his way around the coffins, looking for something to prize the lids off. In the first coffin there is nothing of interest, save for the dust which billows around. In the next coffin he pushes back the coffin lid, and to his horror sees* DRACULA *laying out on a pile of new soil. Music crescendo.)*

HARKER   The Count! The Count looking half renewed. The cheeks fuller, and the white skin ruby-red underneath. The mouth redder than ever, and on the lips great drops of fresh blood. It seemed like the whole creature was simply gorged with blood. He lay like a filthy leech, exhausted with his repletion. But there was no sign of movement, no pulse, no breath, no beating of the heart. A terrible desire came over me. To end the world of such a monster!

*(*HARKER *finds a workman's shovel. He picks it up and makes his way towards the coffin with* DRACULA *in it. Silence.* HARKER *moves above the coffin. Suddenly* DRACULA *opens his eyes and looks up at* HARKER, *who screams.* DRACULA *reaches up for* HARKER. *Loud music plays. Blackout. Lights rise on* DOCTOR SEWARD'S *asylum. Howling, banging, screaming.)*

SEWARD   Oh Lucy, dearest Lucy.

VOICE   *(distorted)* Lucy, Lucy.

SEWARD   I do not eat, I cannot rest, I cannot sleep, I can think only of dearest Lucy. I went down amongst the one who has afforded me a study of much interest. He is so quiet in his ideas, and so unlike the normal lunatic, that I am determined to understand him as well as any man can. R M Renfield. Sanguine temperament; great physical strength;

morbidly excitable periods of gloom ending in
some fixed idea which I can't make out.
Probably dangerous, to himself and others.
Lately his hobby has been catching flies. He
has such a quantity that I myself have to
expostulate. But recently he has turned his
mind to spiders, and has got several very big
fellows in a box.

VOICE 3   Dr Seward . . . Dr Seward.

SEWARD   He keeps feeding them with his flies, and the
number of the later is becoming sensibly
diminished. His spiders however are
becoming an even greater nuisance than his
flies, and I told him he must get rid of them.

               (RENFIELD *enters. He is wearing the garb of
               institution.*)

RENFIELD   No. Never.

SEWARD   Every last one. They are a disgrace.

RENFIELD   They are wholesome and good for me.

SEWARD   I fear not sir.

RENFIELD   They are full of life. Strong life, and they
give me life, Dr Seward. They give life to me.

SEWARD   Do they?

RENFIELD   They do sir, but I would happily rid myself of
them if you were to do me a favour Doctor,
sir.

SEWARD   Would you?

RENFIELD   Oh I would sir.

SEWARD   What favour could I do you Mr Renfield?

RENFIELD   I would like a kitten sir.

SEWARD	A kitten.
RENFIELD	Oh yes sir, a nice little sleek playful kitten, that I can play with and teach, and feed and feed and feed!
SEWARD	A kitten?
RENFIELD	Sir!
SEWARD	Would you not rather have a cat?
RENFIELD	A cat?
SEWARD	A cat.
RENFIELD	Oh yes I would like a cat. I only asked for a kitten lest you should refuse me a cat. No one would refuse me a kitten would they sir?
SEWARD	No sir.
RENFIELD	Oh a cat sir, yes please sir, a cat. A lovely cat. A lovely fat cat.
SEWARD	I fear at the moment that this is not possible.
RENFIELD	Yes.
SEWARD	I'm sorry.
RENFIELD	A cat sir. I want a cat Dr Seward, and I want it now. Now! Do you here me I want it now! I want a cat now!
	(RENFIELD *becomes uncontrollable. He begins to shout and wail. Two hospital attendants come to him and restrain him. He is taken off stage.* SEWARD *addresses the audience.*)
SEWARD	I gave him a strong opiate, and took away his pocketbook in which he makes copious notes. The man is an homicidal maniac. I have

invented a new name for him, a zoophagous
maniac. A life-eating maniac, what he desires
is to absorb as many lives as he can. He gives
many flies to one spider, and many spiders to
one bird, and now wants a cat to eat the many
birds. It would be almost worthwhile to
contemplate vivisection. Why not advance
science in it's most difficult and vital aspect
— the knowledge of the brain?

(*Music.* SEWARD *exits.* LUCY *enters. She is
sleepwalking.* MINA *follows her on stage. She
lights a candle and looks around for* LUCY.)

MINA   Lucy? Lucy?

(LUCY *continues to sleepwalk. There is a
slightly erotic quality to her movement, free
and carefree.* MINA *is aloft upstage. She is
caught in the candle light.*)

MINA   I left the house where we had been sleeping
            and ran up along the North Terrace, but could
            see no sign of the white figure which I
            expected.

(*A* SAILOR, *caught in a gale, speaks out to the
audience.*)

SAILOR   Bloody hell, has tha seen bloody sea? Waves
            as high as ten men and a mist tha could cut
            through. It's out there, look at it, it's being
            tossed about like sommat not right. The
            Demeter isn't it? I'm glad I'm not on that
            bugger, bloody hell!!!

(*He exits.* MINA *moves towards another raised
area upstage.*)

MINA   At the edge of the West Cliff across the pier I
            looked across the harbour to the East Cliff, in
            hope or fear — I didn't know which — of
            seeing Lucy in our favourite seat. Lucy?
            Lucy? Lucy?

(*Music.* Lucy *is now prostrate as mist looms on stage. A large black figure comes to* Lucy *and bends over her. She puts her arms around the neck of the figure, and they embrace.* Lucy *screams out, it is almost orgasmic.*)

MINA   Lucy?

(*The figure exits.* Mina *comes down stage to* Lucy *who is asleep and breathing heavily.* Lucy *is attempting to get her breath. She is struggling to catch air in her lungs. She pulls her nightdress up around her throat. Her breathing calms down.* Mina *takes off her shawl and pins it around* Lucy's *shoulders. She appears to make a slight nick in* Lucy's *neck.* Lucy *winces.*)

MINA   Shhhh . . . shhhh . . .

(*A spotlight rises on* Seward, *upstage.*)

SEWARD   A strange and sudden change in Renfield last night. At about one o'clock he began to get excited and sniff about as a dog does when setting.

LUCY   Mina. Oh Mina!

SEWARD   All he would say was, he didn't want to speak to me now. 'Now that the Master is at hand.' I wonder if he has been seized by some sort of religious mania.

LUCY   So cold now.

SEWARD   I found him pressed close against the door of the old chapel, apparently talking to someone.

(Renfield *in spotlight, upstage.*)

RENFIELD   I'm here Master, I am here to do your bidding Master.

LUCY   Mina . . . help me . . .

RENFIELD   I shall be patient, Master.

                (RENFIELD *makes a deafening silent scream.*)

SEWARD   He is calmer now. His cries are at times
                awful, but the silences that follow are more
                deadly still, for he means murder in every
                turn and movement. I was too excited to
                sleep, but this diary has quieted me. I feel at
                last that I might get some sleep.

                (SEWARD *exits.* MINA *brings* LUCY *to her feet.*
                LUCY *walks and languidly reclines on a*
                chair.)

MINA   I don't understand Lucy, she eats well and
                sleeps well, and enjoys fresh air; but all the
                time the roses from her cheeks are fading, and
                she gets weaker. At night I hear her gasping
                as if for air. I now keep the key of our door
                always fastened to my wrist at night, but she
                gets up and walks about the room, and sits at
                the open window. She has two small marks on
                her neck, the size of a pin prick. I know one
                of them is made from my clumsiness. But
                they are still open, and if anything larger than
                before. They are like white dots with red
                centres. Unless they heal within a day or two
                I will insist on her seeing a doctor.

                (LUCY *stands and comes down stage.*)

LUCY   Mina.

MINA   What is it?

LUCY   Just what you have been waiting for?

MINA   Jonathan?

LUCY   It must be, look at the post mark.

MINA	Jonathan?
LUCY	Aren't you going to open it?
	(MINA *opens the letter.*)
MINA	My hands are shaking.
LUCY	So, what does he write?
MINA	The poor fellow has been ill.
LUCY	Ill?
MINA	Mr Hawkins has written of him. I am to leave in the morning and to go over to Jonathan and to help to nurse him and bring him home. Mr Hawkins says it would not be a bad thing if we were to be married out there.
LUCY	Ah . . .
MINA	He has been suffering a violent brain fever, and the dear Sister Agatha at the hospital of St Joseph's in Budapest has been caring for him. Sister Agatha has written to Mr Hawkins on Jonathan's behalf.
LUCY	You must go to him Mina, you must go at once.
MINA	But what of your illness here?
LUCY	I am fine. Believe me, I am absolutely fine!
MINA	But I have my work at the school.
LUCY	You must go to Hull, board a ship, and dash immediately to Jonathan.
	(*A musical sting.* LUCY *exits.* MINA *reads.*)

MINA   Dearest Lucy, I know that you will be anxious
            to hear all that has happened since we parted
            at the railway station at Whitby. Well my
            dear, I got to Hull all right, and then the boat
            on to Hamburg and then the train on to here.

            (HARKER *enters, in a wheelchair. He is clearly
            extremely weak. Silence.*)

MINA   Oh please God . . .

HARKER   I'm fine. Fine.

MINA   What happened?

HARKER   I don't know if what I have seen is true or if I
            am becoming a madman. You know I have
            had brain fever.

MINA   The Sister said so.

HARKER   And you know to have brain fever is to be
            thought of as mad.

MINA   Darling, don't even think of it!

HARKER   I am not mad, Mina. I tell you. Not mad.
            What I saw is the truth. It is here. (*He lifts
            aloft a small notebook.*) I made note of
            everything. I do not want to know it. I must
            start my life again, anew, with our marriage.
            Keep this book, take it, read it if you will, but
            never let me know; unless, indeed, some
            solemn duty should come upon me to go back
            to the bitter hours, asleep or awake, sane or
            mad recorded here.

MINA   I will keep the book Jonathan, and it will be a
            sign that all our lives we will trust each other.
            And I will never open it unless for your poor
            sake.

            (MINA *is crying.*)

Dracula's Voice	A stranger in a strange land. I have come to know much about your great England. And to know her is to love her.

(*Laughter.* Lucy *enters.*)

Lucy	Dearest Mina, Oceans of love and millions of kisses and may you soon be back home with your new husband.

(Mina *and* Harker *exit.*)

The strong air would soon restore Jonathan: it quite restored me. I was full of life but since I have returned home I have taken to walking in my sleep once more. Perhaps it is the change of air, or returning home again. I feel horribly weak, I am ghastly pale and my throat pains me. I have not told Arthur. I try to cheer up when I see him or else I know he will be miserable to see me so. By the way I forgot to tell you Arthur is here. There he is calling me. No more from me. Your ever-loving Lucy. PS. Mother sends her love. PPS. We are to be married September 28th.

(Seward *enters.*)

Seward	Madam Lucy.
Lucy	Arthur is still in the drawing room.
Seward	That's why I came in here.
Lucy	Please!
Seward	Sorry.
Lucy	I'm already spoken for.
Seward	I'm sorry.
Lucy	So you should be.

SEWARD   A moments weakness that's all. I wanted to
              see you alone.

LUCY   I am always alone Jack.

SEWARD   Indeed?

LUCY   Always.

SEWARD   Are you not well?

LUCY   Perfectly thank you.

SEWARD   A little pale.

LUCY   A doctor might not be so forward.

SEWARD   But perhaps a friend might be?

LUCY   Perhaps.

SEWARD   Arthur looks well. Your mother must be
              feeding him.

LUCY   Her health isn't all it should be.

SEWARD   He told me.

              (*A beat.*)

              Oh Lucy . . .

LUCY   Oh Jack, we have been having such fun.
              Walks and drives and rides and rowing and
              tennis, and fishing. I think I love Arthur more
              than ever. Is that awful of me?

SEWARD   What?

LUCY   Speaking of it like this?

SEWARD   How could it be?

LUCY   I'm sorry . . .

SEWARD	Don't be.
LUCY	Are you well?
SEWARD	Devastated.
LUCY	Don't be silly.
SEWARD	I mean it.
LUCY	Arthur tells me that he loves me more than I love him but I doubt that could be possible. Do you think?
SEWARD	I'm just pleased that you're both very happy.

(ARTHUR *enters*.)

ARTHUR	Extremely happy, old chap. And that's that.
SEWARD	Lucy was just telling me what a wonderful time you're having.
ARTHUR	Heaven, dearest Jack. Heaven itself.
SEWARD	It certainly sounds like it.
LUCY	So what are we to do today?
ARTHUR	Rest perhaps.
LUCY	He's tired, aren't you?
ARTHUR	She tires me to death, bless her.
LUCY	Am I too gay, Arthur?
ARTHUR	I don't know, what do you think Doctor?
SEWARD	I think it isn't prudent for a man to say too much in front of an husband to be.
ARTHUR	Very well said.

LUCY   Coward.

SEWARD   Completely, madam.

LUCY   You must stay for tea Jack Seward, Mama
                expects to speak with you later.

SEWARD   I will of course.

                (LUCY *exits. Silence.*)

                You are a lucky man, Arthur Holmwood.

ARTHUR   I know it.

SEWARD   Indeed so.

ARTHUR   Very lucky.

SEWARD   Indeed.

ARTHUR   Jack?

SEWARD   Yes.

ARTHUR   How is she do you think?

SEWARD   Who?

ARTHUR   Lucy.

SEWARD   Why?

ARTHUR   Is she ill?

SEWARD   Pale maybe but . . .

ARTHUR   Help me Jack. I know I'm no doctor. She has
                no special disease, but she looks awful.

SEWARD   Well . . .

ARTHUR   It's getting worse every day. You remember
                how she used to look? I am sure there is
                something praying on the poor girl's mind. I
                am almost beside myself when I think of her;
                even to look at her gives me a pang of
                sickness.

SEWARD   Have you spoken with her?

ARTHUR   I told her I should ask you to see her, and at
                first she was, well . . .

SEWARD   I understand.

ARTHUR   It will be a painful task for you, old friend.
                But I ask you to do it.

SEWARD   Perhaps she should see someone else.

ARTHUR   Please Jack. Please, for her sake.

SEWARD   When would you have me see her?

ARTHUR   Now.

                (*The entire cast laugh and chat gaily. A light
                minuet plays.* LUCY *enters, she is laughing
                and sits on a chair posing.* ARTHUR *sits nearby
                and stoically listens.* SEWARD *addresses the
                audience.*)

SEWARD   Later that evening we dined, and Lucy
                seemed to me fine and gay and full of life. I
                went with her to her boudoir and as soon as
                the door was closed, the mask of gaiety fell
                from her face and the poor girl sank into a
                chair with a great sigh.

LUCY   I cannot tell you how I loathe all this talking.

SEWARD   Everything you say to me is . . . /

ARTHUR   / . . . Lucy we are anxious about you.

LUCY   I am fine, I just need rest, I need sleep. You
            know what it's been like lately.

ARTHUR   Just stay calm.

SEWARD   (*to audience*) I could easily see now that she
            was, as Arthur had observed, somewhat
            bloodless. But she doesn't appear to have the
            usual anaemic signs.

ARTHUR   Well that's good, isn't it?

SEWARD   Do you feel any pains at all?

LUCY   My breathing. I have difficulty getting my
            breath. I feel lethargic, heavy. And dreams.
            Oh Doctor Jack Seward, what dreams!

SEWARD   Are they dreams you can remember?

ARTHUR   Dreams?

SEWARD   Lucy?

ARTHUR   Lucy, can you speak of these dreams?

LUCY   They are frightening, sick, ugly dreams.
            Dreams I cannot speak of.

ARTHUR   What do you mean? What kind of dreams?
            What kind of dreams can't she speak of?

SEWARD   Arthur I beg you . . .

LUCY   When I was a child I used to walk in my
            sleep. When I was with Mina in Whitby the
            habit came back. It was the night of the
            storm.

SEWARD   Storm?

ARTHUR   Did you not hear of it? The Demeter from
            Varna was forced into the harbour up there.

The only thing to come off the ship was a dog. Where the dog went God only knows.

SEWARD   Good grief.

ARTHUR   The Captain had strapped himself to the wheel. All the crew were missing. Dead.

SEWARD   Good lord!

ARTHUR   Maybe it is this that makes her dream?

SEWARD   It doesn't sound very scientific.

LUCY   You know I love you don't you?

           (*They move away from* LUCY.)

ARTHUR   What is it Jack? What is wrong with her?

SEWARD   I am in some doubt.

ARTHUR   Doubt?

SEWARD   She seems to me to be in a normal state of physical health. In her physical matters I can assure you that there is no need for anxiety.

LUCY   I am perfectly well. I told you.

SEWARD   But I will do what I think is best.

ARTHUR   Which is?

SEWARD   I will write to my old friend and master.

LUCY   There is no need.

SEWARD   He knows as much about obscure diseases as anyone in the world.

ARTHUR   And?

SEWARD   I will ask him to come over. I am only too
                happy to do anything for Lucy that I can, and
                I know that he will do anything for me.

ARTHUR   Is he a doctor?

LUCY   I don't need another doctor. No, no, no!

SEWARD   He is without question one of the most
                advanced scientists of his day. He has an
                absolutely open mind. And though he appears
                rather arbitrary he knows what he is talking
                about better than anyone else I know.

ARTHUR   Who is he Jack?

SEWARD   He is Abraham Van Helsing.

ARTHUR   Van Helsing!

SEWARD   Professor Van Helsing from Amsterdam!

                (*Music.* VAN HELSING *comes forward. He is
                backlit.* ARTHUR *retreats upstage.*)

VAN HELSING   Have you said anything to the lover?

SEWARD   No.

VAN HELSING   Quite right. Better he not know what might
                lay ahead.

SEWARD   What do you think it might be?

VAN HELSING   Ah my good friend John, you deal with the
                madmen.

SEWARD   Indeed I do but . . .

VAN HELSING   All men are madmen in some way or another.
                And you deal with your madmen in one way.
                So the world deals with God's madmen in
                another. You tell not your madmen what you
                do, nor why you do it. So you and I will keep

our thoughts here and here. I have for myself
thoughts on what you have told me. Later I
shall unfold them to you in the fullness of
time. Now, take me to the young lady so that
I might make a diagnosis.

(*Music.* LUCY'S *room.* LUCY *lays on the bed.*
VAN HELSING *and* SEWARD *arrive at her*
bedside. VAN HELSING *examines her.*)

VAN HELSING   My God, this is dreadful! There is no time to
be lost. She will die for the sheer want of
blood to keep her heart's action as it should
be. There must be transfusion of blood at
once! Is it you or me?

SEWARD   I am younger, Professor. It must be me.

VAN HELSING   Then get ready at once. I am prepared.

(RENFIELD *is caught in a spotlight upstage.*)

RENFIELD   (*screaming*) The Master is here! He is
coming . . .

(RENFIELD *sits. The light goes out.* ARTHUR
enters. He is anxious.)

ARTHUR   Professor Van Helsing, I wanted to thank you
for coming. How is she?

VAN HELSING   Sir, you have arrived just in time. You are the
lover of the Miss?

ARTHUR   Yes, of course.

VAN HELSING   She is bad, very very bad.

ARTHUR   Oh my God.

VAN HELSING   Sir, you are to help her. You can do more than
any alive and your courage is your best help.

ARTHUR   What can I do? Tell me and I shall do it. My
                    life is hers and I would give the last drop of
                    blood in my body for her.

VAN HELSING   I do not ask as much as that.

ARTHUR   As what?

VAN HELSING   The last drop.

ARTHUR   What shall I do?

VAN HELSING   Come. You are a man, and a man is what we
                    want. The young Miss is bad, very bad. She
                    wants blood, and blood she must have or die.
                    My friend John and I have consulted and we
                    are to perform what we call a transfusion of
                    blood — to transfer from full veins of one to
                    empty veins that pine for him. John was to
                    give blood, as he is more young and strong
                    than me — but now you are here, you are
                    more good than us, old or young, who toil so
                    much in the world of thought. Our nerves are
                    not so calm and our blood not so bright as
                    yours.

ARTHUR   If you only knew how gladly I would die, you
                    would understand.

VAN HELSING   In the not so far off you will be pleased you
                    have done all for her you love. Come now and
                    be silent. You shall kiss her once before it is
                    done, but then you must go and you must
                    leave at my sign. (*They approach* LUCY.) Now
                    Miss, here is your medicine. Drink it all, like
                    a good child. See I lift, it is easy for you to
                    swallow. Yes. You may make that one little
                    kiss whilst I bring over the table. Friend John,
                    help to me please.

                    (SEWARD *assists* VAN HELSING.)

                    He is so young and his blood so strong and
                    pure that we need not defibrinate it.

(SEWARD *speaks to the audience, whilst* VAN HELSING *operates.*)

SEWARD   Then with swiftness, but with absolute method, Van Helsing performed the operation. The loss of blood on Arthur was telling. When all was over I could see how much Arthur was weakened.

VAN HELSING   The brave lover I think deserves another kiss, which he shall have.

(ARTHUR *kisses* LUCY.)

You must now go home and rest. Sleep much and eat much, then you may be recruited of what you have given to your love. I can tell you sir that the operation has been successful. You have saved her life this time, and you can go home and rest easy in mind that all that can be is. I shall tell her all when she is well; she shall love you nonetheless for what you have done. Goodbye.

(ARTHUR *exits upstage.*)

SEWARD   A bold man.

VAN HELSING   Ah yes. But dearest John. What do you make of the mark on her throat?

SEWARD   What do you make of it?

VAN HELSING   I can make nothing of it. As yet. I must go back to Amsterdam, tonight.

SEWARD   Tonight?

VAN HELSING   There are books and things which I want. You must remain here all night, and you must not let your sight pass from her.

SEWARD   Shall I have a nurse?

VAN HELSING   We are the best nurses, you and I. You keep
               watch all night. See that she is well fed and
               that nothing disturbs her. You must not sleep
               all night. Later on we can sleep, you and I. I
               shall be back as soon as possible and then we
               may begin.

SEWARD   May begin? What on earth do you mean?

VAN HELSING   We shall see.

               (*A spotlight picks out* RENFIELD. *Again he is
               screaming.*)

RENFIELD   Yes, yes a cat, a cat would be good sir. A nice
               big cat.

               (*A musical sting. Light out on* RENFIELD. VAN
               HELSING *exits upstage. As he does a* MAID
               comes to SEWARD.)

MAID   May I not sit up with Miss Lucy sir?

SEWARD   No, I.

MAID   I pray you, may I not watch over Miss Lucy,
               doctor?

SEWARD   I'm afraid not. Dr Van Helsing wishes that
               only I stay with her.

MAID   Please sir!

SEWARD   I'm sorry but thank you. Miss Lucy will be
               much touched by your kindness.

MAID   Sir.

               (*The* MAID *returns upstage.* SEWARD *sits with*
               LUCY.)

SEWARD   You must sleep.

LUCY	I'm afraid to.
SEWARD	Afraid to sleep?
LUCY	Yes, yes, terribly afraid.
SEWARD	Why so? It's what we all crave for.
LUCY	Not if you are like me . . . if sleep was to you a presage of horror!
SEWARD	A presage of horror! What on earth do you mean?
LUCY	I don't know. And that is what is so terrible. All this weakness comes to me in sleep. Until I dread the very thought.
SEWARD	But my dear girl you may sleep tonight. I am here watching you, and I can promise that nothing will happen.
LUCY	Dearest Jack.
SEWARD	And I promise you that if I see any evidence of bad dreams I will wake you at once.
LUCY	Will you?
SEWARD	At once.
LUCY	How good you are to me.
SEWARD	Then sleep, Miss Lucy. Just sleep.

(LUCY *falls asleep. A musical tone.*)

All night long I watched by her. She never stirred, but slept on and on in a deep, tranquil life-giving, health-giving sleep. Her lips were slightly parted and her breast rose and fell with the regularity of a pendulum. There was a smile on her face, and it was evident that no bad dreams had come to disturb her peace of mind. For two nights I hardly had a wink of sleep.

LUCY   No sitting up for you tonight Jack.

SEWARD   No, I'm fine . . . honestly.

LUCY   You are completely exhausted. And I am quite well again and if there is to be any sitting up then I shall be the one who does it, in looking after you.

(VAN HELSING *comes down stage.*)

VAN HELSING   So, the Miss is better already?

LUCY   Much better Professor, but dearest Jack is dog tired. The poor man hasn't had a wink of sleep for two whole nights.

(VAN HELSING *offers* LUCY *a bunch of white flowers — garlic.*)

VAN HELSING   These are for you Miss Lucy.

LUCY   For me?

VAN HELSING   Yes, my dear, but not for you to play with. These are medicines. They are not to take in concoction form, so you need not snub that charming nose. This is medicinal but you know not how. I put him in your window, and hang him around your neck, so that you sleep well.

LUCY   Around my neck?

VAN HELSING   Then you shall sleep.

LUCY   I believe Professor Van Helsing that you are playing a joke with me. These flowers are nothing more than common garlic.

VAN HELSING   Yes.

LUCY   Is this a joke?

VAN HELSING   I never joke. There is good purpose in all I
                do; and I warn you, do not thwart me. Take
                care for the sake of others if not your own.

LUCY   Jack, what does he mean?

VAN HELSING   Do not fear. I only do for you good; there is
                much virtue for you in these so called
                common flowers.

SEWARD   Well there is always reason in what the
                Professor does Lucy, but I have to admit that
                this puzzles me. It is just as well we have no
                sceptic here, or he would say you were
                working out some spell to keep out an evil
                spirit.

VAN HELSING   Perhaps I am.

SEWARD   What?

VAN HELSING   Take care you do not disturb, and even if the
                room feels close, do not tonight open the
                window or the door.

LUCY   I promise. And thank you a thousand times. I
                don't know what I have done to be blessed by
                such friends.

VAN HELSING   Have a good night Miss Lucy. I must rest
                myself. Two nights of travel, and much
                reading have left me exhausted. I will return
                to see you tomorrow.

                (VAN HELSING *and* SEWARD *exit.* LUCY *falls to
                sleep.*)

VOICES   The dead travel fast, the dead travel fast, dead
                travel fast.

(Music. The MAID *enters stealthily. She sees* LUCY *asleep, and smells the strong garlic. She makes a move over to the garlic and collects most of it together.* SEWARD *comes down stage. As he does the* MAID *freezes.* VAN HELSING *is in tow. The* MAID *exits upstage. Silence.* VAN HELSING *raises his arms and makes a frustrated gesture.)*

VAN HELSING   Ah man! God! God! God! What have we done. What has this poor thing done that we are so beset? Why are all the powers of the devils against us?

SEWARD   Devils?

VAN HELSING   Come we must operate again.

SEWARD   But Professor . . .

VAN HELSING   Is the lover not presently available?

SEWARD   Arthur is with his dear father Lord Godalming, who has taken ill. He did promise to return on Tuesday.

VAN HELSING   In that case I shall provide the blood. Make yourself ready.

*(*SEWARD *and* VAN HELSING *exit upstage and freeze.* LUCY *addresses the audience from her reclined position.)*

LUCY   So, four days and nights of peace. I am getting so strong that I hardly know myself now. It is as if I have passed through some long nightmare, and had just wakened to the beautiful sunshine. And since Dr Van Helsing has been with me, all this bad dreaming seems to have passed away, the noises that used to frighten me out of my wits — the flapping against the windows, the distant voices which seemed so close to me, the harsh sounds that came from I know not where and commanded

me to do I know not what — have all ceased.
I go to bed without any fear of sleep. I have
grown quite fond of garlic, and a box arrives
for me every day from Haarlem. Tonight Van
Helsing has returned to Amsterdam. But I
need not be watched for I am well enough to
be left alone.

(*Music, as* LUCY *returns to her reclining
position.* RENFIELD *is caught in a spotlight. He
is straight-jacketed.*)

RENFIELD   The blood is the life, the blood is the life,
             Master. I am waiting. I am waiting Master!

             (*Light out on* RENFIELD. *The* MAID *comes down
             stage.*)

MAID   Miss Lucy went to bed as usual, placing the
             flowers as Dr Van Helsing had directed.

RENFIELD   Aaaahh. Aaaahh.

MAID   It appeared that she tried to go to sleep but
             could not.

LUCY   Is anyone there?

             (*A howling is heard, off stage.*)

MAID   There was no sound but the howl of a dog.

LUCY   Is anyone there?

MAID   She looked against the window but could see
             nothing.

LUCY   Except a big black bat, which had been
             buffeting it's wings against the window.

MAID   She returned to bed once more.

LUCY   Hello? Who is it? Is there anyone there?

MAID   There was a howl again and then a crash at
                 the window. Broken glass was hurled to the
                 floor and the head of a big grey wolf appeared
                 in the window.

                 (LUCY *screams. More howls are heard
                 outside.*)

MAID   The air seemed full of specks, floating and
                 circling in the draught from the window.

LUCY   God help me, God help me. Goodbye dear
                 Arthur, if I do not survive this night. God
                 keep you dear.

                 (*The* MAID *returns upstage.* LUCY *is still.*
                 SEWARD *rushes down stage with* VAN HELSING
                 and ARTHUR. VAN HELSING *goes to* LUCY.)

VAN HELSING   Mine Gott! She is dying. It will be much
                 difference mark me, whether she dies
                 conscious or in her sleep.

ARTHUR   Lucy! My God, Lucy.

LUCY   (*weakly*) Arthur. I am so glad you have come.

ARTHUR   I'm here dearest.

LUCY   Kiss me.

ARTHUR   Lucy dear, rest.

LUCY   One last kiss.

                 (LUCY's *breathing becomes heavy.*)

                 My love kiss me, please kiss me.

                 (ARTHUR *goes to kiss* LUCY. LUCY *is lustful.
                 She snarls and grabs him strongly. She is
                 about to bite his neck. There is a huge
                 commotion.* VAN HELSING *fights to break* LUCY
                 from ARTHUR.)

VAN HELSING	Not for your life!
	(LUCY *is now back to herself. She takes* VAN HELSING'S *hand and kisses it.*)
LUCY	Guard him, and give him some peace.
VAN HELSING	I swear it. Come sir, take her hand and kiss her on the forehead only once.
	(ARTHUR *comes and kisses* LUCY *gently on the forehead.* ARTHUR *steps back and* LUCY *calmly dies.*)
VAN HELSING	It is over. She is dead.
ARTHUR	Oh God! Oh God Jack, Jack, what shall I do? The whole of life seems gone from me now. There is nothing, nothing in the world left for me to live for!
SEWARD	There is peace for her at last. Poor girl. Poor, poor Lucy.
ARTHUR	Oh Lucy . . . dear God! Dear dear God.
	(ARTHUR *exits upstage. He is beside himself.*)
SEWARD	At last it is the end.
	(*A beat.*)
VAN HELSING	Not so Jack.
SEWARD	What?
VAN HELSING	Alas she is not at peace. And it is not the end.
SEWARD	What are you saying?
VAN HELSING	It is only the beginning.
SEWARD	The beginning?

VAN HELSING   Tomorrow I want you to bring me a set of
              post mortem knives.

SEWARD   Must we make an autopsy?

VAN HELSING   Yes and no. I want to operate, but not as you
              think.

SEWARD   Good grief man!

VAN HELSING   You are shocked, ah! A surgeon! You who I
              have seen, without a tremble of hand or heart,
              do operations of life and death which would
              make others shudder?

SEWARD   Professor I beg you not to do this.

VAN HELSING   Ah, do I forget that your friend John, did love
              her?

SEWARD   I beg you not to do this.

VAN HELSING   Ah John . . .

SEWARD   In all that is right and proper . . .

VAN HELSING   I have not forgotten, and you must help. We
              will do the operation after the coffin lid has
              been screwed down. Then we can unscrew it,
              and none will know.

SEWARD   But why do it at all? The girl is dead. Why
              mutilate her poor body without need?

VAN HELSING   There are things that you do not know. But
              you shall know. They are not pleasant things.
              And you have never known me do anything
              without good cause.

SEWARD   But there is nothing to gain by it. Is there?

VAN HELSING   Yes . . . yes.

SEWARD   Professor Van Helsing?

VAN HELSING   I have good reason. And if I work without you
                I work with a heavy heart and feel lonely.

SEWARD   If there is nothing to gain for science, for her,
                for humanity, it is just monstrous. I beg you
                Professor, don't do it.

VAN HELSING   There are strange and terrible days before us.
                Let us not be two, but one, that so we work to
                a good end. You must have faith in me?

                (*Blackout. A strong musical chord.* SEWARD
                and VAN HELSING *exit upstage.* LUCY *is
                cleared.* MINA, *dressed for a funeral, comes
                down stage.*)

MINA   Such a sad blow has befallen us. Mr Hawkins
                has died very suddenly. Some may not think it
                so sad for us but we had both come to so love
                him that it really seems that we have lost a
                father. And since arriving back in Exeter from
                Budapest Jonathan is greatly distressed. It is
                not only that he feels great and deep sorrow
                for a man who treated him like a son but also
                because we have made our home with Mr
                Hawkins and been very happy indeed.

                (VAN HELSING *is held in a spotlight upstage.*)

VAN HELSING   Dear Mrs Mina Harker. You will be grieved to
                hear that five days ago Miss Lucy Westenra
                died. Her mother Mrs Westenra also died of a
                failed heart. There is a wealth of sorrow in
                these few words. God save us all.

                (*Music — "Abide With Me".* VAN HELSING,
                MINA, HARKER, SEWARD. *They are gathered for*
                LUCY's *funeral. All of them are dressed in
                black, with suitable rain cover. A tableau is
                established as they sing a verse of "Abide
                With Me". As the tableau breaks up* VAN

HELSING *establishes contact with* MINA. *The rest of the cast retreat upstage*.)

VAN HELSING   Mrs Harker is it not, that was Mina Murray? I am Dr Van Helsing. It is on account of poor dear Lucy that I must speak with you.

MINA   Sir, you could have no better claim on me than that you were a friend and helper of Lucy Westenra.

VAN HELSING   Can we speak frankly?

MINA   I think we can Professor.

VAN HELSING   I know you were at Whitby.

MINA   That is right.

VAN HELSING   I understand that sometimes Lucy kept a diary.

MINA   She did.

VAN HELSING   And in that diary she talks of her sleep walking along a cliff and you saving her.

MINA   That is true.

VAN HELSING   I wonder then if you would be so kind as to tell me what you remember.

MINA   I can remember everything, doctor.

VAN HELSING   Ah, very good. It is not always so with young ladies.

MINA   I am a school teacher, Dr Van Helsing, and I took the precaution of noting all that Lucy told me in a small note book. I am not like all young ladies.

VAN HELSING   So it appears. May I read the note book?

MINA   If you wish.

VAN HELSING   Where is it?

MINA   I have it safe at home.

VAN HELSING   Good. Then perhaps I can see it.

MINA   If you wish.

VAN HELSING   And your husband is quite well? I understand
                he has had a fever? Has all that gone?

MINA   Almost. We were in town a few days ago and
                he had another onset of the fever. It was a
                kind of shock I think.

VAN HELSING   A shock. That was not good. What kind of
                shock was it?

MINA   We were walking in Piccadilly when he
                thought he saw the gentleman he'd been
                working with in Europe.

DRACULA'S   I love your London. Its life. Its death.
VOICE

VAN HELSING   And was it him?

MINA   Jonathan didn't know, poor thing. He said it
                looked like him, but then he said it couldn't
                be because the gentleman looked so much
                younger.

VAN HELSING   Younger?

MINA   Yes. Rather as if the older he got the younger
                he looked. I must confess Doctor that I am
                quite worried by Jonathan.

VAN HELSING   I will be glad to help you.

MINA   I'm afraid he may be still suffering.

VAN HELSING   If your husband suffer, he suffer within the
               range of my study and experience. I promise
               you that I will gladly do all I can for you and
               him, to make him strong and manly once
               more.

MINA   Dr Van Helsing, what I have to tell you is so
               strange that you must not laugh at me or my
               husband.

VAN HELSING   My dear, if you only knew how strange the
               matter regarding which I am here it is you
               who would laugh. I have learned not to think
               little of anyone's belief, no matter how
               strange.

MINA   My Husband kept a journal when he was in
               Transylvania.

VAN HELSING   Transylvania?

MINA   I dare not say anything of it.

VAN HELSING   Madam Mina, I will read it, and I will come
               to see you and your husband.

MINA   When?

VAN HELSING   Tomorrow.

               (*Music.* VAN HELSING *exits upstage,* HARKER
               brings a large note book to VAN HELSING.
               MINA *and* VAN HELSING *sit with* HARKER. *They
               are in* HARKER'S *drawing room.*)

HARKER   I fear Doctor that you may think me a fool . . .

VAN HELSING   Some might say.

HARKER   I am no fool Doctor . . .

VAN HELSING   I know sir. I know. You may sleep without
               doubt of that, because strange and terrible as
               it is, it is the truth.

MINA   Oh, thank God.

VAN HELSING   The truth Madam.

MINA   A thousand thanks. You have taken a weight
                off my mind.

VAN HELSING   The truth.

MINA   But if it be true, what terrible things are there
                in the world, and what an awful thing if that
                man, that monster, be really here in London!

HARKER   Dr Van Helsing, I didn't know what to trust. I
                was even beginning to distrust my own
                senses.

VAN HELSING   We must be friends. We must be friends all
                our lives and keep the dark secrets within our
                hearts. But I must ask you for more help.

HARKER   Does what you have to do concern Count
                Dracula?

VAN HELSING   It does.

HARKER   Then I am with you Dr Van Helsing, heart and
                soul.

                (*Blackout. Music.* MINA *and* HARKER *retreat
                upstage.* SEWARD *comes down stage. He is at
                the asylum.* VAN HELSING *rushes to him with a
                copy of the Westminster Gazette.*)

VAN HELSING   Have you seen this?

SEWARD   Good grief man are you mad, making a fellow
                jump so?

VAN HELSING   The paper, the paper.

SEWARD   What of it?

VAN HELSING	Read it.
SEWARD	What is it?
VAN HELSING	Children are being decoyed away at Hampstead. Read the passage about their throats.
SEWARD	(*reads*) Small punctured wounds appeared on the throats of two young girls . . .
VAN HELSING	Mien Gott!
SEWARD	Like poor Lucy . . .
VAN HELSING	And what do you make of it?
SEWARD	Simply that there is some cause in common. Whatever it was injured her, injured them.
VAN HELSING	That is true indirectly, but not directly.
SEWARD	How do you mean Professor?
VAN HELSING	Do you mean to tell me, friend, that you have no suspicions of what Lucy died of?
SEWARD	Of nervous prostration following on great loss or waste of blood.
VAN HELSING	And how was the blood lost?
SEWARD	Well I . . .
VAN HELSING	I suppose you do not believe in corporeal transference?
SEWARD	What are you saying?
VAN HELSING	No? Nor in materialization? Nor in astral bodies? Nor in the reading of thought, or hypnotism?
SEWARD	Well yes, Charcot has proved that very well.

Van Helsing	There are always mysteries in life.
Seward	To be proved Professor.
Van Helsing	Can you tell me why, in the Pampas, there are bats that come at night and open the veins of cattle and horses and suck their veins dry? How in some islands of the western seas there are bats which hang on the trees all day, that those who have seen describe as like giant nuts or pods, and that when the sailors sleep on deck, because it is that hot, flit down on them, and then — and then in the morning are found dead men, white even as Miss Lucy was.
Seward	Do you mean to tell me that Lucy was bitten by such a bat? That such a thing is here, in London in the nineteenth century?
Van Helsing	Can you tell me how the Indian fakir can make himself to die, be buried, have his grave sealed, corn sowed on it and then men take away the unbroken seal and the fakir rise up and was as before?
Seward	Professor let me be your pet student again. Tell me the thesis that I may apply your knowledge as you go along.
Van Helsing	My thesis is this — I want you to believe.
Seward	Believe what?
Van Helsing	To believe in things that you cannot.
Seward	What do the Americans say: faith enables us to believe in things we know to be untrue.
Van Helsing	You think that those small holes in the children's throats were made by the same that made holes in Miss Lucy?

SEWARD   It is possible.

VAN HELSING   But you are wrong. Oh would it be so. It is
                worse . . . far worse.

SEWARD   In God's name Professor Van Helsing, what
                do you mean?

VAN HELSING   Much much worse.

SEWARD   Good God man.

VAN HELSING   Exactly.

SEWARD   What is it you are saying?

VAN HELSING   They were made by Miss Lucy.

SEWARD   Are you mad?

VAN HELSING   Would that I were.

SEWARD   My God!

VAN HELSING   Madness would be easy to bear compared to
                truth like this.

SEWARD   This is absolute madness itself!

VAN HELSING   Tonight I go to prove it.

SEWARD   How?

VAN HELSING   Dare you come with me?

SEWARD   To do what?

VAN HELSING   First that we go now and see the child in the
                hospital. Dr Vincent, of the North London
                Hospital is a friend of mine. He will let two
                scientists see his case, that is all. We shall
                tell him nothing. Only that we wish to learn.

SEWARD   And then, Doctor?

VAN HELSING   We spend the night, you and I, in the church yard where Lucy lies.

SEWARD   Good lord!

VAN HELSING   This is the key that locks the tomb. I had it from the coffin man to give to Arthur.

SEWARD   And then what do you intend to do?

VAN HELSING   To open the coffin. Take out the poor girl's heart, and cut off her head!

SEWARD   My God!

               (LUCY *makes a sickening scream. Music. Blackout.*)

ACT TWO

*Music. A coffin is placed downstage centre. The actors enter
as the the music fades. Silence.*

*VAN HELSING, SEWARD and ARTHUR make their way very slowly
to the coffin. A number of lanterns light their way. The
silence is deafening. As they near the coffin we hear the
hollow sound of voices laughing in the distance. VAN HELSING
takes out a screw driver, and very slowly and carefully he
unscrews the coffin.*

ARTHUR	What are we doing here man? This is madness!
SEWARD	Professor are you sure we're . . .
LUCY'S VOICE	The dead travel fast.
DRACULA'S VOICE	I love your London.
ARTHUR	This is desecration of the grave sir!
VAN HELSING	There are mysteries that men can only guess at. Believe me we are now on the verge of one.
	(VAN HELSING *slides back the coffin lid. Silence. The coffin is empty.*)
ARTHUR	Good Lord . . .
SEWARD	Just as you predicted.
ARTHUR	Is this your doing?
VAN HELSING	I swear to you by all that I hold sacred I have not touched her.
SEWARD	Where is the body?

ARTHUR   Is this some joke sir?

VAN HELSING   No joke, my friend.

ARTHUR   Is this some mistake?

VAN HELSING   No mistake.

ARTHUR   Then what does it mean?

                (*A number of voices scream, and wail.
                Upstage we see* LUCY. *She is dressed all in
                white. She has drops of blood on her breast.*
                ARTHUR, VAN HELSING *and* SEWARD *are
                transfixed as they see her. She is still very
                wanton.*)

LUCY   Come to me Arthur. Leave these others and
                come to me. My arms are hungry for you.
                Come to me and we shall rest together. Come
                my husband . . . come.

ARTHUR   Oh my God Lucy!

LUCY   Come my darling, make love to me, come . . .

                (ARTHUR *is about to move to* LUCY *when he is
                caught by* VAN HELSING, *who holds a crucifix
                in front of her. She gasps. The voices upstage
                (*MINA/DRACULA) *also recoil and gasp as a
                chorus.* VAN HELSING *forces* LUCY *back into
                her coffin, where she lies as if asleep.
                Silence.*)

VAN HELSING   Answer me my friend, am I to proceed in my
                work?

ARTHUR   Do as you will. There can be no horror like
                this any more.

SEWARD   Is this really Lucy's body or some demon in
                her shape?

VAN HELSING   It is her body, yet it is not. In a while you
               will see her as she was.

SEWARD   But it is almost as if she is sleeping.

VAN HELSING   The Undead can only move at sundown, in the
               darkness and in the shadows. She rests now
               and we my friends must not waste time.

ARTHUR   Poor Lucy.

VAN HELSING   Lucy suffers the curse of immortality. Forced
               to go on age after age, adding new victims
               who then themselves become Undead. The
               circle widens. Arthur, if you had met that kiss
               before poor Lucy died, you would in time
               have become a nosferatu.

               (DRACULA *gasps*.)

SEWARD   So what of the children in the hospital?

VAN HELSING   Those children are not yet so bad. If she die,
               who did suck their blood, then their wounds
               disappear.

SEWARD   Can you be sure Doctor?

               (VAN HELSING *digs into his bag. He brings out
               a very sharp stake and a large hammer.*)

VAN HELSING   We can never be absolutely sure. Never.

ARTHUR   And what will come of Lucy?

VAN HELSING   Her soul shall be free. It will be a blessed
               hand for her that shall strike a blow and set
               her free.

ARTHUR   Tell me what I must do and I shall not falter.

VAN HELSING   We must drive a wooden stake through her
               heart.

ARTHUR   My God!

VAN HELSING   A fearful ordeal, but it will be done in a short time.

ARTHUR   Oh Lucy.

VAN HELSING   You must place the point of this stake over the heart. Then when we begin our prayer for the dead, strike in God's name, so that all may be well with the dead that we love, and that the undead pass away.

                (ARTHUR *takes the stake.* VAN HELSING, SEWARD, ARTHUR *and* MINA *begin to say a prayer.* ARTHUR *begins to strike the stake.* LUCY *screams, writhes and howls.* DRACULA *responds too. The noise is slowly rising.* ARTHUR *is working hard hitting the stake. He is frenzied and falls from the coffin, crying.*)

ARTHUR   Oh my God, Lucy, Lucy.

VAN HELSING   You may kiss her, my friend. For she is not a grinning devil now — not any more. She is God's true dead.

                (ARTHUR *regains his composure and kisses* LUCY.)

                Now you must go, there is still work to be done here, and I must work alone.

                (ARTHUR *and* SEWARD *exit upstage and freeze.* VAN HELSING *feels inside his bag and takes out a saw. He turns to the coffin.* MINA, ARTHUR *and* SEWARD *all cry out. He begins to saw.*)

DRACULA   Lucy, my child. So sweet. So so sweet and innocent. And now gone!

MINA
SEWARD   }   No, no no. Professor!!!
ARTHUR

MINA   Lucy! Lucy!

                (*Music. The coffin is cleared. A spotlight hits*
                VAN HELSING, *who turns and addresses the*
                audience.)

VAN HELSING   The head comes off so easily. So, so easily.
                Now one step of our work is done. But there
                remains a greater task; to find the author of
                all this sorrow and to stamp him out. I have
                clues which we will follow but it is a long
                task, and difficult, there is danger and pain in
                it. Tonight I leave for Amsterdam, but I shall
                return tomorrow.

                (VAN HELSING *exits.* SEWARD *enters and*
                addresses the audience.)

SEWARD   On my return from that horrible scene I found
                a telegram waiting in my study. It was from
                Mina Harker.

DRACULA'S   Ah, Mina.
VOICE

SEWARD   She is to come up and stay with us at Carfax.
                Where she will impart some important news.

                (MINA *comes downstage.* SEWARD *sits.*)

MINA   We need have no secrets amongst us; we must
                work together with absolute trust, we can
                surely then be stronger than if some of us
                were in the dark.

SEWARD   You say your husband is still in Whitby?

MINA   Yes he thought it best to return, to make as he
                says . . .

                (HARKER *comes into a spotlight whilst the*
                others freeze.)

HARKER   On the spot enquiries. It was now my object
                  to trace that horrid cargo from the Demeter to
                  its place in London. There were fifty boxes of
                  common earth, to be used for experimental
                  purposes. The boxes were main and mortally
                  heavy. Mr Billington was good enough to give
                  me the name of his old companion, the station
                  master at King's Cross. I was able to ask him
                  about the arrival of the boxes. By good
                  fortune I discovered from the foreman that the
                  boxes had left King's Cross to be delivered to
                  Purfleet. There is one thing I am now
                  satisfied; all the boxes which arrived at
                  Whitby from Varna in the Demeter were
                  safely deposited in the old chapel at Carfax
                  Abbey.

                  (*The light goes out on* HARKER. SEWARD *and*
                  MINA *become animated.*)

SEWARD   Good Lord, here at Carfax?

MINA   I wonder whilst we wait for the Professor if
                  you could illuminate me with some of your
                  work here? It is safe, isn't it?

SEWARD   Good Lord of course. We use the very latest
                  in psychological developments. I wouldn't
                  expose one such as yourself were it not safe.

                  (RENFIELD *becomes animated upstage.*)

RENFIELD   Or a spider, or a bird, a bird would do very
                  nicely Dr Seward.

SEWARD   Let us start, if we may, with Mr Renfield. The
                  man is an absolute lunatic.

RENFIELD   Let her come Dr Seward, please please. I'll
                  put my spiders away, please Doctor.

                  (RENFIELD *enters. Lights.* MINA *and* SEWARD
                  are now down in the asylum. RENFIELD *is
                  calmer now, almost sane.*)

MINA   Good evening.

RENFIELD   Evening.

MINA   Dr Seward has spoken of you.

RENFIELD   You're not the girl the doctor wanted to
            marry, are you?

MINA   No I . . .

RENFIELD   You can't be, you know. She is dead.

MINA   I have a husband of my own.

RENFIELD   Uhhh!

MINA   I was married to him before I ever saw Dr
            Seward. I am Mrs Harker.

RENFIELD   And very nice too, may I say.

MINA   No you may not.

RENFIELD   What're you doing here then?

MINA   I'm visiting the Doctor . . .

RENFIELD   Don't.

MINA   I beg your pardon?

RENFIELD   Don't stay here. Go. Go.

MINA   Go?

RENFIELD   Go now! Don't stay here.

MINA   Why not?

SEWARD   How did you know that I wanted to marry
            anyone?

RENFIELD   What an asinine question!

MINA   I don't see that at all.

RENFIELD   You will of course understand, Mrs Harker,
                that when a man is loved and honoured as our
                host is, everything regarding him is of interest
                in our little community.

MINA   Quite so.

SEWARD   I am flattered.

RENFIELD   The Doctor has strange and wonderful beliefs.
                I am myself an insistence of a man who had a
                strange belief. It was no wonder that my
                friends were alarmed, and insisted on my
                being put under control. I used to fancy that
                life was a positive and perpetual entity, and
                that by consuming a multitude of living
                things, no matter how low in scale of
                creation, one might indefinitely prolong life.
                At times I held the belief so strongly that I
                tried to take human life. Isn't that the case Dr
                Seward? Dr Seward . . . Dr Seward . . .

                (SEWARD *turns and speaks to the audience.*)

SEWARD   I hardly knew what to say. It was hard to
                imagine that this man had been eating up his
                spiders and flies not fifteen minutes previous.
                And yet here he was making absolute sense.

MINA   Goodbye Mr Renfield, and I hope that I may
                see you often, under circumstances pleasanter
                to yourself.

RENFIELD   Goodbye my dear. I pray God I may never see
                your sweet face again. Ever. May he bless you
                and keep you. Goodbye. Goodbye, goodbye.
                Goodbye.

                (RENFIELD *exits upstage. A musical sting.*
                MINA, *a* NURSE, HARKER, VAN HELSING *and*

SEWARD *take chairs and form a small meeting group centre stage. The* NURSE *sees the group. Throughout this,* DRACULA *slowly prowls, half-lit, upstage.*)

VAN HELSING   I may, I suppose, take it that we are all acquainted with the facts that are in these papers? Papers prepared and annotated by Mina Harker and from her husband's journal. I think now that I should tell you something of the enemy with which we have to deal. There are such beings as vampires; some of us have evidence that they exist. I admit that at first I was sceptic. But I have tried, through long years, to keep an open mind. The nosferatu does not die like the bee, he gets stronger and stronger, more power to work more evil. This vampire which is amongst us is as strong as twenty men; he can also, within his range command all the elements — fog, thunder, storm . . .

DRACULA   Ah, yes.

VAN HELSING   He can grow, and he can become small; at times he can vanish and become unknown. But we too have strength on our side. We have the resources of science; we have the hours of the day and the night equally. Let us consider the vampire we seek. He cannot pass running water at the slack or the flood of the tide. And there are things which so affect him that he has no power — the garlic, that we know of . . . the crucifix. There are others, too. A sacred bullet fired into his coffin. A stake through the heart, or indeed as we did with Madam Lucy, to cut off his head.

MINA   Oh My God! (*She begins to cry.*)

DRACULA   Mina, lovely Mina.

VAN HELSING   Thus when we find this creature in his habitation we must confine him to his coffin

and destroy him. We have here much data,
and we must proceed to lay out our campaign.
We know much. It seems to me that we must
ascertain where the remaining boxes lay in
the Abbey beyond the wall, or whether some
of them have been removed. If they have, we
must trace them. But I must say that now for
you Madam Mina, this night is the end of
your playing a part, till all is well. You are
too precious for us all to risk. When we part
tonight, you must question no more. We are
men, and we are able to bear, but you must be
our star and our hope, and we shall act all the
more free because you are not in danger. As
there is no time to lose I vote that we look at
his house right now. Time is everything with
him and swift action on our part might save
another victim.

(*The men stand to leave.* MINA *sobs gently.
The* NURSE *hands* SEWARD *a note.* SEWARD
speaks to the audience.)

SEWARD   Just as we were to leave the house an urgent
                message was brought to me from Renfield . . .

                (RENFIELD *comes downstage. The* NURSE, VAN
                HELSING, MINA *and* HARKER *depart upstage and
                sit. Lights change.* RENFIELD'S *cell in the
                asylum.*)

RENFIELD   Dr Seward please, let me out of this asylum at
                once.

SEWARD   Renfield . . .

RENFIELD   Ask not why, just let me depart Doctor. Send
                me away, how you will and where you will,
                send keepers with me, send me in chains and
                straight-jacket, manacled, iron-legged, even
                to jail, but let me out of this house sir. Now!

SEWARD   Mr Renfield?

RENFIELD   Now! Now! You don't know what you do by
                keeping me here.

SEWARD   I cannot send you . . .

RENFIELD   I am speaking to you from the depths of my
                heart, of my very soul. Take me out of this,
                man. Can't you hear me? Can't you see
                reason in this? Will you never learn? Don't
                you know that I am sane and earnest now; that
                I am no lunatic in a mad fit, I am a sane man
                fighting for his soul, let me go!

SEWARD   No more of this, we have had quite enough
                already.

RENFIELD   Let me go.

SEWARD   Go to your bed, and try to behave more
                discreetly.

RENFIELD   I warned you of this, I warned you!

SEWARD   Go to bed man!

                (RENFIELD *makes his way upstage*.)

RENFIELD   No . . . no . . . I am no lunatic, am I no
                lunatic. Tell Madam Mina I am no lunatic!

                (HARKER *and* VAN HELSING *come down stage.*
                MINA *is caught in a spotlight. The action is
                seamless.*)

MINA   Jonathan? Jonathan is that you?

HARKER   We made our way to the house taking care to
                keep in the shadows of the trees.

MINA   Jonathan?

VAN HELSING   Keep this near your heart.

                (VAN HELSING *hands out a small crucifix*.)

MINA	Jonathan? Hello? Dr Jack?
VAN HELSING	I will also need this, for enemies more mundane.
	(VAN HELSING *reveals a revolver*.)
RENFIELD	By all you hold dear, by all love that is lost, let me out of here tonight!
MINA	(*whispers*) Jonathan . . .
SEWARD	The walls of Carfax Abbey were fluffy and heavy with dust, in the corners were masses of spider's webs.
VAN HELSING	You know this place Jonathan?
MINA	Jonathan?
VAN HELSING	Which is the way?
	(VAN HELSING, HARKER *and* SEWARD *take a step forward*.)
HARKER	As we entered the chapel we were prepared for some unpleasantness.
RENFIELD	(*crying*) Please . . . please . . . please . . .
HARKER	But none of us ever expected such an odour as we encountered. It was composed of all the ill of morality and with the pungent acrid smell of blood.
VAN HELSING	Twenty nine boxes were left. Twenty nine left out of fifty.
SEWARD	We found nothing. Nothing in the chapel, save dust, dust in extraordinary proportions.
	(VAN HELSING, SEWARD *and* HARKER *rest for a while*.)

VAN HELSING   So it seems that he has gone elsewhere.

                   (RENFIELD *laughs*.)

VAN HELSING   It has given us the opportunity to cry 'check'
                   in some way in this chess game which we play
                   for the sake of human souls. Dawn is close at
                   hand, we have reason I think, to be pleased
                   with this night's work.

RENFIELD   Out, out. Let me out Dr Seward. Let me out!

                   (HARKER *addresses the audience. The others
                   retire*.)

HARKER   The next morning I contacted Thomas
                   Snelling, who was responsible for transferring
                   the boxes of earth from Carfax. He told me he
                   had taken six cart loads to Chicksand Street,
                   Mile End New Town, and another six to
                   Jamaica Lane, Bermondsey. But what of the
                   other boxes from Varna? Snelling told me that
                   Sam Bloxam's wife might help down in
                   Pincher's Alley.

                   (MRS BLOXAM *enters. She is very cockney*.)

MRS BLOXAM   Far as I can reckon they made two journeys
                   between Carfax and a house in Piccadilly.
                   They took nine boxes by a horse and cart.
                   Heavy an' all as I reckon.

HARKER   Can you tell me the number of the house in
                   Piccadilly, Mrs Bloxam?

MRS BLOXAM   Narr, I forgets the numbers, but it was only a
                   few doors from a big white church or
                   something. It was dusty an' all. Though not as
                   dusty as the bloomin' place we got 'em from.

HARKER   How did you and your men get into the houses
                   if they were empty?

MRS BLOXAM	There was the party what engaged us waiting in the house at Purfleet. He helped my lot lift the boxes into a dray. You should've seen him, I ain't never seen a man so strong, and him getting on in years an' all. I wish my old man had had that type of strength. My boys were a puffin' and blowin' and he lifts it like a box of tea.
HARKER	But how did you get into the house in Piccadilly?
MRS BLOXAM	He was there too.
HARKER	He got there before you?
MRS BLOXAM	He must have set off in advance or something. For when I rung the bell he opened the door himself. And we left nine boxes there in the hallway. There was nothing else in the house.

(DRACULA *laughs, off.*)

HARKER	Did you ever have a key?
MRS BLOXAM	No never did, never had a key or nothing. He just opened the door and in we went.
HARKER	And you cannot remember the number of the house?
MRS BLOXAM	No, but it's high with a stone front, and high steps to the door.
HARKER	Thank you, thank you very much.
MRS BLOXAM	I thought you said something about reimbursement?
RENFIELD	(*calling from upstage*) Dr Seward? Dr Seward?

(MRS BLOXAM *goes to sit upstage.* HARKER *addresses the audience.*)

HARKER   At Piccadilly Circus I discharged my cab, and
              walked westward; beyond the junior
              constitutional I came across the house
              described, and was satisfied that this was the
              next of the lairs arranged by Dracula.

VOICE 1   For your mother's sake don't go in.

VOICE 2   Take a crucifix.

VOICE 3   Denn die todten reiten schnell . . .

HARKER   The windows were encrusted with dust and
              the shutters were up. Behind the rails of the
              balcony a 'For Sale' sign. Perhaps Mitchell,
              Sons and Candy, the house agents, could tell
              me something?

              (*The* AGENT *enters from upstage.*)

AGENT   It is sold sir.

HARKER   Pardon me Madam, but I have a special
              reason for wishing to know who purchased it.

AGENT   It is sold sir.

HARKER   Surely you don't mind . . .

AGENT   I am sorry sir, but the property is sold.

HARKER   I wonder if you could supply me . . .

AGENT   The affairs of their clients are absolutely safe
              in the hands of Mitchell, Sons and Candy.

HARKER   Your clients, Madam, are happy in having so
              resolute a guardian. I am myself a
              professional man. In this instance I am not
              prompted by curiosity; I act on the part of
              Lord Godalming who wishes to know
              something of the property.

AGENT   I would like to oblige you if I could . . .

HARKER   Madam I . . . ?

AGENT   The original vendors are the executors of the
                 late Mr Archibald Winter-Suffield. The
                 purchaser is a foreign nobleman, Count de
                 Ville, who affected the purchase himself,
                 paying the purchase price in notes, 'over the
                 counter'. Beyond this we know nothing
                 whatsoever.

                 (*The* AGENT *retires upstage.* HARKER *addresses
                 the audience.*)

HARKER   Doubtless we are on the trail of the missing
                 boxes. If we find them all in that house then
                 our work is near an end. I returned home to
                 Purfleet to find my beloved Mina tired and a
                 little paler than usual.

                 (HARKER *exits upstage.* RENFIELD *becomes
                 restless. He moans and hurls himself around
                 the stage.*)

RENFIELD   No, no. No, I can't stand it please, please,
                 please, Dr Seward! Dr Seward? Please Doctor.
                 Doctor.

                 (*Blackout on* RENFIELD *as he falls stage
                 centre. The* NURSE *screams. Music.* SEWARD
                 rushes downstage. He speaks to the audience.)

SEWARD   An attendant from the asylum came bursting
                 into my room. Renfield had somehow met
                 with an accident. She had heard him yell, and
                 when she went to him found him lying on his
                 face on the floor.

                 (VAN HELSING *comes downstage to* SEWARD.)

VAN HELSING   Friend John, how is he?

SEWARD   The face is bruised, as though it has been
                beaten against the floor many times. I think
                his back is broken. His right arm and his leg
                and the whole side of his face are paralysed.

VAN HELSING   How could such a thing happen?

SEWARD   I can't understand the two things. He could
                mark his face like that by beating his own
                head against the floor. I have seen that done
                before. And he might break his back by
                falling out of bed, but the two things
                together?

VAN HELSING   A sad accident.

                (RENFIELD *begins to stir*.)

RENFIELD   What is wrong with my face?

VAN HELSING   Careful.

RENFIELD   My face, Doctor . . .

VAN HELSING   Tell us what happened man, tell us your bad
                dream . . .

RENFIELD   It was no dream.

SEWARD   What happened man?

RENFIELD   No dream. But all grim reality.

VAN HELSING   Tell us what happened.

RENFIELD   Doctor, I am dying. I feel that I have but a
                few minutes, then I must go to death or worse.

VAN HELSING   Tell us . . .

RENFIELD   The night . . . the night after you left me . . .
                you should have let me go away Doctor, let
                me go. I couldn't speak then, but I was sane, I
                was sane. My brain seemed cooler. I heard the

dogs bark behind our house, but not where he was.

VAN HELSING   Go on.

RENFIELD   He came up to the window as mist. I had seen him like that before, his eyes, his eyes laughing at me.

(VOICES *laugh, off.*)

His red mouth, his shall white teeth. He began promising me things, not in words but by doing them.

VAN HELSING   How?

RENFIELD   By making them happen, just as he used to send in the flies when the sun was shining. Great big fat ones, with steel and sapphire on their wings; and big moths in the night with skull and crossbones on their backs. (*Whispers.*) Rats, rats, rats, hundreds, thousands, millions of them, a dark mass spread over the grass. And he held up his hand and said, "all these will be yours if you will fall down and worship me". I knew what I was doing, I opened up to him and said come Lord and Master. Then all day I waited to hear from him, but he didn't contact me . . . nothing from him, not even a blowfly. Then he came in and went by me, he didn't even smell the same, it smelt as if Mrs Harker had come into my room. And she wasn't the same; it was like tea when the teapot had been watered. She didn't look the same.

SEWARD   Good Lord man what are you saying?

RENFIELD   It made me mad to know that he was taking her . . .

SEWARD   This is just . . .

RENFIELD   Yes, he was taking her, taking all the life out
                of her. I tried, I tried for Mina . . . I told you
                Doctor.

SEWARD   Poor Mina.

RENFIELD   I have heard that madmen have much
                strength. It was no good, when his eyes
                burned at me my strength turned to water.

                (VOICES *laugh, off.*)

                There was a red cloud before me, and a noise
                like thunder, and the mist seemed to steal
                away under the door.

VAN HELSING   He is here, and we know his purpose.

SEWARD   Alas, that dear Mina should suffer.

VAN HELSING   We must make straight for Mina and
                Jonathan's room.

RENFIELD   I warned you, Doctor . . . I warned you . . .

                (*Music. In a dream-like slow motion,* HARKER
                and MINA *prepare for bed.* MINA *wears a
                nightdress. Both begin to settle but* MINA
                *cannot. She wakes, and moves down stage, as
                if in a half-trance.* SEWARD *and* VAN HELSING
                try to make their way as in a dream to the
                HARKER'S *bedroom. They are upstage, slow
                motion.* DRACULA *comes slowly downstage.*
                DRACULA *and* MINA *meet while* HARKER *sleeps
                in a chair.* MINA *is completely entranced by*
                DRACULA. *He takes* MINA'S *head and holds it
                strongly. She is suppliant. He forces her face
                into his breast. He makes her lick his breast.
                She is both excited and disgusted.* DRACULA *is
                just about to devour* MINA *when* SEWARD *and*
                VAN HELSING *enter.* DRACULA *recoils, throwing*
                MINA *to the floor.* VAN HELSING *fumbles for a
                small crucifix which he drops on the floor.*
                SEWARD *stumbles to collect it and* VAN

HELSING *holds up the cross.* DRACULA *recoils.*
He exits upstage. VAN HELSING *and* SEWARD
attempt to help MINA. *Music stops.* MINA *is in*
a frenzy, she is acting as if she has been
raped. Her breathing is heavy, she is wild.
VAN HELSING *comforts her. Slowly she regains*
normal breathing. SEWARD *wakes* HARKER, *who*
is startled by the scene.)

HARKER   In God's name, Dr Seward, Professor . . .
            what has happened? Has it come to this?
            Good God man, help us, help her! Dr Van
            Helsing do something to save her. It cannot
            have gone too far yet. Guard her whilst I look
            for him.

MINA   No, Jonathan, you must not leave me. I have
            suffered enough for tonight. You must stay
            with me. Stay with these friends who will
            watch over you.

HARKER   My heart sinks for you.

MINA   Oh darling Jonathan, forgive me please,
            please forgive me . . .

HARKER   Forgive you?

MINA   Is it a sin Jonathan? Is it a foul filthy sin?

HARKER   Professor . . . ?

MINA   I have tasted him.

HARKER   Mina please . . .

MINA   I have tasted evil, have I not? I have tasted
            evil. Is it a sin, to have these feelings?

            (VAN HELSING *hands* MINA *the small crucifix.*)

VAN HELSING Do not fear. We are here, and whilst this is
            close to you no foul thing can approach. You

	are safe for tonight. And we must be calm and take counsel together.

MINA   I am unclean. I must touch him or kiss him no more. And yet I want to.

HARKER   Mina?

MINA   I am unclean, and now his worst enemy.

HARKER   Mina, Mina, nothing will ever come between us.

MINA   I kissed his mouth, I felt his breath. I tasted him on my tongue. Oh that I would die!

VAN HELSING   No, you must live! You must struggle and strive to live. You must fight death himself, though he come to you in pain or in joy, in day or in night. Do not think of death until this great evil is past.

MINA   I promise you, that if God will let me live, I will strive to do so. But my heart beats so when I think of the evil within him.

VAN HELSING   It is perhaps well that after our visit to Carfax we did nothing with the earth boxes which lay there. Had we done so the Count would have guessed our purpose.

VAN HELSING   We have now this full day to hunt him out.

HARKER   Then let us go, and destroy the boxes at Carfax and Piccadilly . . .

VAN HELSING   Mina you are quite safe here until the sunset. But before we go let me see you armed against personal attack. Take this Sacred Wafer. In the name of the father, the son and the . . .

(MINA *places the wafer on her forehead, as she does she screams. In the darkness* DRACULA *screams with joy.*)

MINA   Arrgghh, it's burning!

DRACULA   (*laughing*) Burning, burning away all your sins, pretty Mina.

MINA   Even the Almighty shuns my polluted flesh. I must bare this mark of shame upon my flesh until Judgement Day . . .

HARKER   If Mina be a vampire in the end she will not go to the grave alone Dr Van Helsing, promise me that.

VAN HELSING Friend John . . .

HARKER   (*shouts*) Promise me . . .

VAN HELSING Mr Harker . . .

HARKER   Promise me!

             (*Music swells. Lights change as* MINA *retires upstage.* HARKER, SEWARD *and* VAN HELSING *create a chevron tableau and speak directly to the audience.*)

HARKER   We entered Carfax without trouble and found all things the same as on the first occasion.

SEWARD   One by one we treated in the same way each of the great boxes, and left them as we had found them but in each was a portion of the Host.

VAN HELSING So much is done already it may be that the sunset of this evening may shine on Madam Mina.

HARKER	We moved then to Piccadilly. Arthur Holmwood and his man had gone to houses in the south and east.
SEWARD	We had news they had destroyed six boxes each.
HARKER	We entered the house through the hall way.
SEWARD	All keeping together in case of attack.
HARKER	In the dining room at the back of the house, we found eight boxes of earth.
VAN HELSING	Eight . . . only eight.
HARKER	Eight out of the nine which we sought.
SEWARD	In each of the boxes of earth we left a portion of the Host.
HARKER	Eight out of nine. There is but one box left and the Count alone knows where it is.
VAN HELSING	Our work is not over until we find the final box. Come, enough for tonight, let us return.
	(They see DRACULA *and all freeze. Music. Slowly* DRACULA *moves downstage. He is behind* SEWARD, HARKER *and* VAN HELSING.)
DRACULA	You think to baffle me Professor?
HARKER	Count Drac —
VAN HELSING	So, we meet at last.
DRACULA	Do you try to baffle me?
VAN HELSING	No sir, I wish to rid the earth —
DRACULA	*You?*
VAN HELSING	Me sir . . .

DRACULA	You with your pale faces all in a row, like sheep in a butcher's shop. You shall be sorry yet, each of you! You think you have left me without a place to rest; I have more, more than you think. My revenge is just begun, and it is spread over centuries. I have time on my side. Your girls that you all love are mine already, and through them you and others will be mine — my creatures, to do my bidding and to be my jackals when I want to feed.
VAN HELSING	Never!
DRACULA	I have had all your lovely girls. You are already too late.

(*Music.* DRACULA *laughs and exits.*)

HARKER	Later that evening Mina called me to her.

(MINA *comes downstage.*)

MINA	Call the Professor, I must see him at once.
HARKER	Are you ill, dearest?
MINA	Call him.
HARKER	Why?
MINA	Call him!
HARKER	What, what is it?
MINA	Call him, please . . .
HARKER	(*to the audience*) Two or three minutes later, Van Helsing was in the room.
VAN HELSING	(*coming downstage*) My dear, what a change. See friend John, we have got our dear Mina back as good as new. And what am I to do for

you? For at this hour you do not want me for nothing.

MINA   I want you to hypnotise me.

VAN HELSING What for?

MINA   Do it before dawn, for I feel then that I can speak and speak freely.

VAN HELSING About what?

MINA   Do it Professor, I feel sure I have some part of me that will speak to you of these dreadful things. Was it not you who said, "believe all is possible?"

VAN HELSING It was . . .

MINA   So please do it. Be quick for time is short.

      (VAN HELSING *takes out a watch.* MINA *watches it.*)

HARKER   (*to audience*) Mina gazed at him fixedly for a few minutes during which my own heart beat like a trip hammer. Gradually her eyes closed till she sat stock still.

      (*A musical tone.*)

VAN HELSING Where are you?

MINA   I do not know. Sleep has a place it can call its own.

VAN HELSING Where are you now?

MINA   It is all strange to me.

VAN HELSING What do you see?

MINA   I can see nothing, it is all dark.

MINA   What do you hear?

MINA   The lapping of water. It is gurgling by, and
                little waves leap. I can hear them outside.

VAN HELSING   Then you are on a ship?

MINA   Oh yes.

VAN HELSING   What else do you hear?

MINA   The sound of men stamping overhead as they
                run about. There is a creaking of a chain, and
                the loud tinkle as the check of the capstan
                falls into the ratchet.

VAN HELSING   What are you doing?

MINA   I am still. It is like death!

HARKER   What does this mean Professor?

MINA   Just like death.

HARKER   Van Helsing?

VAN HELSING   The ship, wherever it is, is weighing anchor
                as she speaks.

HARKER   But there are many ships weighing anchor.

VAN HELSING   Quite so, but which one is it we seek?

HARKER   Seek?

VAN HELSING   The Count means to escape. There is but one
                box left and a pack of men following him like
                dogs after a fox. He has taken his last box
                aboard a ship and he is ready to leave land.

HARKER   But why must we seek him further when he
                has gone away from us?

VAN HELSING   You, friend John, should know this. He can
               live for centuries and Mina is but a mortal
               woman. Time is to be dreaded my friend,
               since he put that mark upon her throat. You
               must stay here. Our enemy has gone back to
               Europe.

               (SEWARD *stands*. HARKER, MINA *and* VAN
               HELSING *remain frozen*.)

SEWARD   (*to the audience*) As we knew that he wanted
               to get back to Transylvania we felt sure that
               he must go by the mouth of the Danube.

DRACULA'S   Velcome to Transylvania.
VOICE

               (*The* NURSE *comes down stage and offers her
               narrative*.)

NURSE   To Lloyds they went first where there were all
               notes of ships however small. There they find
               that the only ship Black Sea bound is the . . .

DRACULA'S   CZARINA CATHERINE . . .
VOICE

SEWARD   Bound from Doolittle's Wharf to Varna.

               (SEWARD *and the* NURSE *retire upstage.* VAN
               HELSING, MINA *and* HARKER *break from their
               freeze*.)

VAN HELSING   So our enemy is on the sea.

HARKER   And the box we seek is bound for Varna?

VAN HELSING   To sail a ship takes time. She does not sail
               quick.

HARKER   When we follow we will go on land.

VAN HELSING   Friend John, you must stay with Madam Mina.
               She is changing.

HARKER   Changing?

VAN HELSING   With the sad experience of Miss Lucy, we
                must this time be warned before things go too
                far. Can you not see the characteristics of the
                vampire coming in her face?

HARKER   I . . .

VAN HELSING   It is now very slight, but is to be seen in the
                eyes.

                (MINA *begins to breath heavily, her breast
                rises and falls. Then she resorts to normality.*)

HARKER   Oh my . . . !

VAN HELSING   Now my fear is this. If it be that she can, by
                our hypnotic trance, tell us what the Count
                see and hear, is it not more possible that the
                Count will make her tell us what he wants us
                only to know.

HARKER   You mean to throw us off the scent?

VAN HELSING   Exactly!

HARKER   So he can speak to Mina and tell her to tell us
                untruths?

VAN HELSING   I fear so.

HARKER   Then what must we do to prevent this?

VAN HELSING   We must keep her ignorant to our intent. So
                she cannot tell what she know not. We must
                tell her she is simply to be guarded by us and
                is not to take counsel. I now leave. The
                Czarina Catherine will take her at least three
                weeks to reach Varna.

HARKER   Three weeks? Think of Mina, it will be too
                late.

VAN HELSING	Seward and myself can travel overland to the same place in three days. You must remain to take care of your sweet wife.
HARKER	Professor let us talk of that hereafter, for now with your permission I need to consult with her.
VAN HELSING	Of course.
	(VAN HELSING *departs and stands aside, as if in another room.*)
HARKER	Mina . . . Mina can you hear me?
MINA	Jonathan, promise me something on your word of honour.
HARKER	What is it?
MINA	A promise made holily to me in God's hearing and not to be broken.
HARKER	Mina, a promise like that cannot be made just at once.
MINA	But dear one it is I who wish it; and it is not for myself.
HARKER	I promise.
MINA	Promise me that you will not tell me anything of your plans to foil the Count. Not by word nor by deed. I fear my fragile state could not bare it. Promise me . . .
HARKER	I promise.
MINA	Where is the Professor?
HARKER	He is to go away.
MINA	And leave us.

HARKER	Mina . . . ?
MINA	We must go with him.
HARKER	Mina?
MINA	We must.

(VAN HELSING *becomes animated*.)

VAN HELSING	Why Madam?
MINA	I am safer with you, and you shall be safer, too.

(DRACULA *laughs, off*.)

MINA	Professor I implore you!
VAN HELSING	Madam your safety is our solemnest duty.
MINA	That is why I must go. I can tell you now, I may not be able to tell you again. I know that when the Count wills me I must go. I know that if he tells me to come in secret then I must come by any device.
VAN HELSING	Madam Mina . . . ?
MINA	I may be of service to you. You can hypnotise me sir and so learn that, which even I myself do not know.

(*Music, "The Final Journey"*. MINA, VAN HELSING, HARKER *and* SEWARD *collect a number of cases. They are stage centre and we get the impression they are caught in a vortex of travelling*.)

HARKER	We left Charing Cross the next morning . . .
SEWARD	Poor Arthur was in no state to make the journey.

MINA	We got to Paris the same night . . .
SEWARD	And took our places on the Orient Express . . .
HARKER	Arrived Vienna early the next morning.
VAN HELSING	We travelled night and day, arriving at Varna at five o'clock.
HARKER	Mina is well, and is looking stronger.
SEWARD	Her colour is coming back.
MINA	Before sunrise and sunset I am wakeful and alert . . .
VAN HELSING	It is at these times that I hypnotise her . . .
HARKER	He always asks what she can see . . .
MINA	Nothing . . .
VAN HELSING	And what can you hear . . . ?
MINA	Waves lapping against the side of the ship . . .
VAN HELSING	He is still at sea.
SEWARD	Four telegrams to me have reported that the . . .
DRACULA'S VOICE	Czarina Catherine . . .
SEWARD	. . . has not yet docked.
DRACULA'S VOICE	The dead travel fast . . .
HARKER	We have already arranged what to do when we reach the box . . .
VAN HELSING	Seward and I will cut off his head and drive a stake through his heart.

SEWARD	His body will then fall into dust.
VAN HELSING	So there will be no evidence against us in case any suspicion of murder were aroused.
HARKER	Murder?
VAN HELSING	Aye, for that is what it is.
SEWARD	The Catherine is reported entering Galatz at one o'clock today.
HARKER	Galatz! I thought he was . . . Galatz?
VAN HELSING	He's escaped us!
SEWARD	Damn . . . Van Helsing?
VAN HELSING	We must take the tram there straight away.
	(*The others freeze as* SEWARD *speaks to the audience.*)
SEWARD	Having acquired authority to make search of the ship as soon as we got there, we continued our journey through the dark hours and into the dawn . . .
HARKER	Nothing, no box, nothing.
VAN HELSING	What do you see Mina?
MINA	Nothing . . .
VAN HELSING	No waves?
MINA	Only water running softly. And voices calling . . .
DRACULA'S VOICE	Come freely. Go safely. And leave some of the happiness you bring.
	(MINA *gasps.*)

HARKER   What is it?

MINA   There is a gleam of light . . . the air is
                  blowing upon me.

VAN HELSING   He is closer now.

SEWARD   He has left his earthly chest.

VAN HELSING   But he has yet to get on shore.

HARKER   Can he not jump or fly as he did at Whitby?

MINA   All is dark, I hear lapping water. Creaking as
                  of wood on wood.

SEWARD   The box from the Czarina Catherine was
                  given to a certain . . .

DRACULA'S   Petrof Strinsky.
VOICE

MINA   Petrof Strinsky?

HARKER   Who dealt with Slovaks and traded downriver
                  to the port.

VAN HELSING   We sought for Strinsky but were unable to
                  find him.

SEWARD   A neighbour told us Strinsky had gone away
                  for two days and no one knew where to find
                  him.

VAN HELSING   We know that he is on the water. The problem
                  is . . .

ALL   What water? And where?

HARKER   I remember that he was taken from the castle
                  by the Svgany, they delivered their cargo to
                  the Slovaks who took the boxes to Varna and
                  shipped them off to London.

SEWARD   So the Count has knowledge of persons who
                could arrange all this . . .

VAN HELSING   When the box was on land, he met Strinsky,
                ordered him to take the box up river, and then
                murdered him, blotting out any traces.

SEWARD   (*whispers*) Murder?

HARKER   The river most suitable for the Slovaks is the
                Pruth or the Sereth.

MINA   The Sereth makes a loop at Bistritz, which
                runs up round the Borgo Pass.

HARKER   This is as near as one can get by water to the
                Castle Dracula.

                (DRACULA *laughs, off.*)

MINA   Van Helsing and I are to leave by the 11.40
                train tonight for Veresti. We will get a
                carriage and drive ourselves to the Borgo
                Pass.

HARKER   Seward and I are to get a steam launch and
                follow the Count up the river.

                (*Lights change. The sound of wind howling as*
                MINA *and* VAN HELSING *affect a carriage.
                Other actors throw snow as they race towards
                the castle.* MINA *and* VAN HELSING *are
                wrapped against the cold night.*)

VAN HELSING   All day long we travelled at good speed.

MINA   It is lovely country here. Full of beauties of
                all imaginable kinds, the people are brave,
                strong and simple.

VAN HELSING   (*to imaginary horses*) Go on yeerr!

MINA   Lapping water, creaking wood.

VAN HELSING   Our enemy is still on the river.

MINA   It is so cold.

VAN HELSING   The country gets wilder as we go, and the
                great spurs of the Carpathians tower before us
                as we go . . .

DRACULA'S   Welcome to Transylvania.
VOICE

MINA   By morning we shall reach the Borgo Pass.

                (*Laughter, howls, noises.*)

VAN HELSING   It seems that the cold has affected Madam
                Mina. She sleeps all day. No chance to
                hypnotise her, for all she do is sleep.

DRACULA'S   You are in the midst of the Carpathians, one
VOICE   of the wildest places in Europe.

VAN HELSING   Up and up and up. All is so wild and rocky as
                though it were the end of the world.

                (MINA *laughs.*)

                And there, there on the steep summit of a hill
                was the castle which Jonathan spoke of in his
                diary. And now I know for good or evil, the
                end is near.

                (MINA *and* VAN HELSING *dismount from the
                imaginary carriage.* VAN HELSING *makes a
                large circle in the ground.* SEWARD *and*
                HARKER *take on the narrative.*)

SEWARD   Van Helsing took out the horses, fed them and
                gave them what shelter he could.

                (SEWARD *retires upstage.*)

HARKER   Then he made a fire, sat Mina near it, and
              drew around the pair of them a large circle.

              (HARKER *retires upstage as* VAN HELSING
              makes a circle.)

VAN HELSING   I make this circle Madam Mina. And over I
              pass some wafer. So we will be well-guarded.
              Will you not eat?

MINA   I am not hungry Professor . . .

VAN HELSING   Are you warm?

MINA   I am fine.

VAN HELSING   You look so pale and cold.

MINA   (*seductive*) Hold me . . .

VAN HELSING   You are cold . . . ?

MINA   Hold me Professor . . . give me some comfort.

VAN HELSING   Madam . . .

MINA   (*seductive*) Hold me, Professor Van Helsing.

              (VAN HELSING *goes over to* MINA. *He touches
              her and she clings to him. She begins to
              shake.*)

VAN HELSING   Will you not sit by the fire?

MINA   I cannot.

VAN HELSING   Why not?

MINA   I cannot.

              (DRACULA *laughs, off.*)

SEWARD   The horses screamed . . .

(VAMPIRES *scream and laugh, off.*)

. . . and tore at their tethers.

(MINA *laughs.*)

(*Music. Upstage, the* VAMPIRE *we saw earlier comes slowly to* VAN HELSING *and* MINA. *She is casual and seductive.*)

VAMPIRE   Come sister . . . come to me sister . . . come to me . . .

VAN HELSING   Madam Mina, do not fear . . .

MINA   I fear nothing Professor.

DRACULA'S   Come to me Mina . . . come to me . . .
VOICE

MINA   Why fear for me . . . there is none safer in all the world than I am.

VAMPIRE   Come Mina . . .

DRACULA'S   Mina come . . .
VOICE

VAMPIRE   Come sister . . .

VAN HELSING   (*screaming*) Back, back . . .

                     (VAMPIRE *laughs and retires upstage.* MINA *falls to sleep.* VAN HELSING *attempts to wake her.*)

VAN HELSING   Mina, Mina! Mina!!

                     (HARKER *and* SEWARD *become animated upstage.*)

HARKER   There has been an accident to the motor launch. We have taken horses and follow on the track.

SEWARD   We ride to the death of someone. God alone
                knows who . . .

HARKER   . . . or where . . .

SEWARD   . . . or what . . .

HARKER   . . . or when . . .

SEWARD   . . . or how it may be . . .

                (*They retire to upstage positions. The* VAMPIRE
                comes once more downstage.)

VAMPIRE   Come sister . . . come to me . . . Are we to
                have no fun tonight Professor? (*Laughs.*)
                Come to me . . . come to me . . .

                (*The* VAMPIRE *freezes,* VAN HELSING *steps into
                a spotlight. He speak to the audience. He is
                fraught with confusion as he speaks.*)

VAN HELSING   There she was, so full of life and voluptuous
                beauty that I shudder at the thought of
                murder. Those beautiful eyes, that breast so
                pure, the mouth, the mouth enticing any man.
                That look of love . . . those lips, the shape of
                the breast rising and falling so gently.

VAMPIRE   Come to me old man . . .

VAN HELSING   With all my motive and yeaning for hate I am
                paralysed and helpless.

VAMPIRE   Come to me . . .

VAN HELSING   Must I kill this creature? So radiant that she
                excites the very instinct in me. She enthrals
                the very soul of me. Oh Mina . . . God be
                thanked that your very cries have not died out
                of my ears. I steal myself to do my wild
                deeds.

VAMPIRE   Come to me . . .

               (*The* VAMPIRE *reacts to each 'stab' from* VAN
               HELSING.)

VAN HELSING   I stab, and stab and stab and stab and stab!
               And that mouth, that pretty mouth, I rip and
               tear open, I rip the flesh, that pretty flesh and
               fill her mouth with foul garlic! Oh my God
               . . . it is a butcher at work. God be thanked
               that my nerve did stand. And as I sever the
               head, that delicate head, which peels from the
               neck the whole body begins to melt away to
               dust, native dust. As though death should
               have come to her centuries ago.

               (VAN HELSING *is quite broken. Lights fade on
               him.* MINA *stands. The* VAMPIRE *melts
               upstage.*)

MINA   My husband is coming towards us.

VAN HELSING   I am a butcher at work.

MINA   Professor?

VAN HELSING   A butcher, no more.

               (MINA *addresses the audience.*)

MINA   In front of us, so near that I wonder why we
               hadn't noticed before, came a group of
               mounted men. In the midst of them was a cart,
               which swept from side to side like a dog's tail
               wagging. It carried on it a large box of earth.
               I knew it was him.

VAN HELSING   They are racing for the sunset.

MINA   Two horsemen followed.

               (SEWARD *and* HARKER *come stage centre.*)

SEWARD   The sun was shining ever more brightly . . .

HARKER   . . . as it sank down behind the mountain
                tops . . .

SEWARD   The cart came to a halt . . .

HARKER   . . . and we were ready.

                (HARKER *and* SEWARD *draw large knives.*
                Music. DRACULA *makes an enormously*
                theatrical entrance down centre.)

DRACULA   So you come now to kill Dracula? You with
                your pale sheep heads. You who cannot even
                hope to love, like I. You who hate the thought
                of a foreigner on your soil! Do you not think I
                know your innermost thoughts? Do you not
                think I know that you all long to be like me,
                to have what you want? To take any woman
                and give her the ultimate satisfaction —
                eternal life? You with your pale sheep faces
                wonder why your women turn from you? (*To*
                MINA.) Ah Mina, you tasted so lovely. And
                now you blush, a big fulsome blush. Why so?

MINA   I . . .

DRACULA   You didn't blush before.

MINA   I erm . . .

DRACULA   And the noises you made?

MINA   Oh . . .

DRACULA   Why are you so taken with these little men? I
                pity you, I pity you all. If, you must kill me
                then come, come now! Do you not know I will
                live forever . . .

                (*Music.* SEWARD, HARKER *and* VAN HELSING *set*
                about DRACULA. *They kick, stab, punch, a*
                revolver shot is heard as mist seeps down
                stage. MINA *screams.*)

MINA   Oh my love . . .

            (HARKER, SEWARD *and* VAN HELSING *have
            become like animals. They are now all
            bloodied and desperate.* DRACULA *walks
            calmly upstage. The rest of the cast are
            gasping for their breath —* VAN HELSING,
            SEWARD *and* HARKER *are speechless.*)

HARKER   Several years ago we all went through the
            flames.

SEWARD   But the happiness we now endure was well
            worth the pain.

MINA   In the summer of this year we made a return
            journey to Transylvania . . .

LUCY   It was almost impossible to believe the things
            we had seen with our own eyes.

HARKER   The castle stands as before . . .

VAN HELSING We want no proofs, we ask no one to believe
            us . . .

SEWARD   Mina's son will some day know what a gallant
            and brave woman she is . . .

HARKER   He already understands her sweetness and
            loving care . . .

VAN HELSING Later on he will understand how some men
            loved her so much that they dare do much for
            her sake.

DRACULA   Oh yes Mina . . . lovely Mina.

            (DRACULA *begins to laugh. The rest of the
            ensemble laugh slightly.* DRACULA *walks
            upstage centre. The rest of the cast follow
            him. They stop with their backs to the
            audience. They turn in unison, and gasp.
            Blackout.*)